Catholic London

by
John Wittich

D1428028

Fowler Wright Books

Dedication

For the Family Ross — Williamson
Hugh, Margaret, Julia and Ross
with grateful thanks for their friendship
over the past four decades.

Catholic London
Contents

iii

Preface

In writing this book the author has delved into Pre-Reformation London and brought to light many interesting facts from that time. The Catholic practices of the time have been re-discovered can be shared by the twentieth century pilgrim.

He has also combined to bring to the attention of modern Londoners the names of those Catholics who gave their lives for the Faith that was so dear to them, and their families.

We should be grateful to him for bringing these interesting facts to our attention and for the loving care that he has taken in gathering them together.

For the modern pilgrim these walks will enable them to stroll through the streets of the City of London, and to recapture something of the splendour of a past age - the Catholic London prior to the schism that caused it to leave the protection of the Pope in Rome.

First published in 1988 by
Fowler Wright Books
Burgess Street Leominster
Herefordshire HR6 8DE

Typesetting by Print Origination (NW) Limited, Formby, Liverpool
Printed and bound in Great Britain by Billings & Son Ltd Worcester

ISBN 0 85244 143 6

Towards the Tower of London
via Southwark.

Towards the Tower of London
—via Southwark

The route from Blackfriars to the Tower of London, via Southwark, takes us through one of the most interesting portions of the City of London. The area contains many places of direct interest to modern Catholics seeking out their heritage in the City.

The starting point for this walk is **Blackfriars Station** (1). Use the subway from the booking hall of the underground station to emerge on the corner of New Bridge Street and Queen Victoria Street. Here can be seen **"The Blackfriar" public house** (2). On the outside of the house stands a number of scenes that show life in the Dominican Priory that once stood near by. Look for the rather contented friar clutching two wine containers, and for the friars fishing for their Friday meal. Inside too, the wall decorations are well worth studying.

Just under the railway bridge turn left into **Black Friar Lane** (3): Note the keystones of the filled in arches of the railway viaduct— they are made of Coade stone, and show the previous occupants of the shops here—a fishmonger, grocer, pharmacist, etc. Walk along until the Society of **Apothecaries' Hall** is reached (4). This Society, one of the livery companies of the City of London was founded in 1617 when they withdrew from their 'mother company' 'the Grocers' and set up a Company on their own—the latter having until that time embraced the drug specialists under their wing. Today the Apothecaries are a flourishing Company all of whom are members of the medical profession. The hall which dates from the 17th century stands on part of the site of a Dominican Friary.

On the corner of Black Friar Lane and Carter Lane is a City Corporation **'blue-plaque'** (5) marking the site of the Dominicans' house from the 13th to the 16th centuries. Founded in London, in 1221 in

1

Chancery Lane by Hubert de Burgh, they moved to this site some fifty years later when Gregory Rokesley, Mayor of London, (1274-1280, and 1284-1285), arranged for them to have five streets near the Thames here. Under royal patronage the friary flourished. It became one of the most important monastic establishments in Pre-Reformation London, with a variety of Council meetings being held here in the medieval City. in 1382. When John Wycliffe, 1324-1384, philosopher Master of Balliol College Oxford, was brought before William Courteney, Archbishop of Canterbury, (1342-1396,) to be examined for his doctrines and Bible translation, the City suffered an earthquake. This was taken by Wycliffe as a sign from God that He approved and that the Church was acting in a wrongful manner against him. The enclosed precinct of the Friary remained a sanctuary long after the Dissolution of the Monasteries Act of 1539, and attracted to it many of the criminal fraternity of the time. At Blackfriars began the Black Parliament in which Cardinal Wolsey, c1475-1530, Archbishop of York and Lord Chancellor was condemned for treason. He died in the abbey at Leicester before he could be brought to trial, and lies buried in a marked grave in the ruins of that abbey today. In the church lay the heart of Queen Eleanor, the first wife of Edward I, 1239-1307, prior to her burial in Westminster Abbey. Also buried here were King James of Spain, 1208-1276, and Sir Thomas Parr, the father of Katherine Parr, the sixth and last 'wife' of Henry VIII, 1491-1547 (she survived him). It was when Parliament met here in 1523, that Saint Thomas More, 1478-1535, was made Speaker of the House of Commons, and as such presided over the House's deliberations here.

From the corner where the plaque is to be found our route takes us along **Carter Lane** (6) as far as **Church Entry** (7). Turn right and walk down the alley-way, pausing to read the noticeboard on the right hand side of the railing which gives a short history of Blackfriars. Here one stands at the junction of the Nave and the Choir of the friars' church. Just past the board there is the Vestry Hall of the former Parish of St. Anne's Blackfriars. This was designed by the late Sir Banister Fletcher, 1866-1953, who served as Senior Sheriff of the City of London in 1919, and co-wrote with his father "A History of architecture on the comparative method" (1896), which is still the "bible" for all architectural students today. The Hall is the sole remains above ground of the former parish, the church of which would have been found outside the gates of the former Blackfriars monastery here.

At the end of Church Entry, is Playhouse Yard: This lies on the site of the refectory of the monastery which in 1539, after the Dissolution, was used as a private theatre for a number of years.

A short walk along Ireland Yard, where William Shakespeare, 1564-1616, once leased a house, leads the walker to St. Andrew's Hill, and the Parish Church of **St. Andrew by the Wardrobe** (8).

The church, situated in Queen Victoria Street, is first mentioned in 1261 in a manuscript now in the archives of St. Paul's Cathedral, it is likely however that there was a church on the site in Saxon times. It's suffix comes from the fact that the King (Edward IV, 1442-1483), having negotiated the sale of Sir John Beauchamp's house here from his executor, used the building to house his wardrobe. After the Great Fire of 1666, the wardrobe was not rebuilt but moved to the Strand. It appears from the records that an extensive library was also established here.

From the church, walk along the roadway until the **College of Arms** is reached (9).

The college founded in 1484 by Richard III, 1452-1485, lost its charter, grants and the house in Cold Harbour Lane after his untimely death at Market Bosworth in Leicestershire on 21st August 1485, in the last important Battle in the War of the Roses. It was not until the time of Philip and Mary that the heralds were reconstituted under a Charter dated 18th July 1555. The College of Arms or Heralds keeps extensive records on the "Arms and Armour" of the Realm. Apart from their work on ceremonial occasions of State which they organise and attend in various official capacities, much of their work consists of tracing and recording pedigrees and establishing right to arms. No one is allowed to display any coats of arms in England unless it has been sanctioned, or produced by the College—Scotland has its own College of Arms in Edinburgh.

The Earl Marshall and Heredity Marshall of England is the Duke of Norfolk, whose family have held the appointment since 1672. By virtue of that office heads the College of Arms although he is not actually a member of the corporation. Like all his forebears the present Duke is a Catholic and is the Premier Catholic Duke of England.

Across the roadway from the College is the Guild Church of **St.**

Benet's (Benedict's) Paul's Wharf (10).
The original church, (the present one dates from after the Great Fire of London in 1666 and was designed by Sir Christopher Wren, 1632-1723,) was known by the name St. Bene't Hithe, doubtless from the small inlet in the river bank here where goods were unloaded. In the fifth act of William Shakespeare's "Twelfth Night", there is a mention of the church viz.
"The Clown (addressing the Duke). The Bells of Saint Bennet,
Sir, may put you in mind,—one, two, three."
As the church was close to Puddle Dock, and the Blackfriars Theatre that Shakespeare founded in the former refectory of the monastery, the bells of the Pre-Fire church would have been very familiar to the playwright. The earliest mention of the church is to be found in a Survey of the Dean and Chapter of St. Paul's in 1181, when it is shown as being St. Benet super Tamisiam or, St. Benet Hude.
Its proximity to Timber Hithe Street the Woodmonger's Hall, may well account for the name being given as St. Benedict de Wudewharf in 1260. The church is associated with one of the oldest Guilds, the Woodmongers'. In 1376 they sent two members of the Company to the Court of Common Council. The Court of Aldermen of the City of London entrusted to the Company the general supervision of all carts and carmen. In 1605 the (Woodmongers with the Carmen) united and became The Worshipful Company of Carmen of the City of London. It was in the Pre-Fire church that the Catholic architect Inigo Jones, 1573-1652, was buried, and his tomb marked by a monument for which he left £100. It was not replaced by Wren when he rebuilt the church in 1683. Today the church serves, the Welsh Episcopalian Church, as it has done since 1879. Services are conducted in the Welsh language every Sunday, morning and evening. The church also serves as the parish church for the College of Arms across the roadway.
Return to Queen Victoria Street and continue to walk along until the church of **St. Nicholas Cole Abbey** is reached (11).
It is unlikely that the church will be open to visitors, unless there has just been, or there is about to commence, a service.
The first mention of the church is in 1144, and the list of Rectors dates back to 1319. The church's suffix "Cole Abbey" comes either from the name of an early medieval benefactor the Colby family, or from the fact that nearby was a Cold Harbour, a sort of medieval

overnight hostel for vagabonds and vagrants, or from the stone cistern in the north wall of the building "for the washing of fish", the result of a bequest from a fishmonger. This doubtless, too, would have been a very cold harbour, particularly in the early hours of the morning when the fish had been unloaded from the boats that had been out all night fishing in the Thames. The latter suggestion makes good sense bearing in mind the fact that the whole parish had become the early fish market of the City. So important was the fish trade to the City and to England in general that Elizabeth I, 1533-1603, insisted that everybody in the land must eat fish on Friday, whether they be Protestant or Catholic. Presumably the English Reformation had brought about a slump in the fish trade following the decline of the practice of eating fish on Friday. Before moving away from the church note the design of the steeple—it is a medieval lighthouse—reminding visitors that St. Nicholas is also the patron of lighthouse keepers, as well as being patron to a number of other persons. It is also worth noting the fact that this parish was the first to restore the Latin Mass after the accession to the throne of Mary I, 1516-1558, on 23rd August 1553. On the following St. Nicholas Day, 6th December, processions were held with the election of the Boy Bishop, but it was not generally practised in the City of London for another two years when we read that St. Mary at Hill bought a book of St. Nicholas and made a mitre "with stuffe and lace that went with yt" for three shillings. With the changing from the Old Faith to the New Faith (Catholic v Protestantism) many of the clergy of the Church in England were faced with a serious dilemma—what to do with their wives. Under Edward VI, 1537-1553, the clergy were allowed to be married and produce offspring, but under the strict ruling of Mary I, 1516-1558, the former Catholic ruling was once again enforced, all married clergymen automatcally divorced. The records show that the parish priest of St Nicholas Cole Abbey sold his 'wife' to a Butcher, for an undisclosed sum of money. "For this he was nicknamed Parson Chicken and pelted with chamber-pots and rotten eggs". His actual name was Thomas Sowdley, despite the accession of Elizabeth I, 1533-1603, and the restoration of the Protestant Creed, he enjoyed the cure of the parish until his death in 1546.

For those wishing to take a short rest there is a pleasant oasis on the opposite side of the roadway to the church. It is the **Fred. Cleary**

Garden, (12) and was opened by Mr Cleary in 1981 as part of the centenary celebrations of the Metropolitan Public Gardens Association.

From the Garden it is a short walk to the **Mansion House Station** (13) and Garlick Hill where can be found the **Parish Church of St. James's Garlickhithe** (14).

St James Garlickhithe

There has been a church on this site since Saxon times, the records show that the church was rebuilt in 1326 by Sheriff Richard Rothing, and that in the same century, in 1375 a religious guild was founded "in worship of Almighty God our Creator, and His Mother. St. Mary, and All Hallows, and St. James Apostle". One of the many persons buried here in the Middle Ages was Richard Lyons, the master of Wat Tyler, the leader of the Peasants Revolt in 1381, Tyler was beheaded by the Lord Mayor of London, William Walworth, after a meeting with the King, Richard II, 1367-1400, at St. John's Meadow (Clerkenwell). All the ancient registers, said to be among the earliest complete set in England, are now safely stored at the Guildhall Library, which dates from 1535. The "sign" of St. James is a scallop shell and examples of this can be found in many places in the church. According to tradition St. James the Apostle was buried in the Spanish town of Compostella. Pilgrims returning from Spain would bring back with them a scallop shell they were once found in abundance there as an indication that they had completed their pilgrimage to his shrine. In later times the shell became the general symbol for pilgrims to wear on and after a pilgrimage to the shrine of a saint. In Pre- Second World War, 1939-1945, days on and around St. James's Day (25th July), the children of London would make a "St. James's Grotto" on the pavements near their homes and ask for "A Penny for the Grotto". Alas this custom seems to have died out completely today. In 1531 Arthur Buckley, the then Rector, was made the Bishop of Bangor, in North Wales, where we read that he sold five of the cathedral bells and was shortly after struck blind. Parochial records show that in 1555 a rood was bought for the parish at a cost of £4.13s.4d., while three years later a rood from a nearby parish, unnamed, was purchased and used to make new pews at St. James's.

From St. James's church it is a short walk to the church of **St.**

Michael Paternoster Royal (15).

Founded in the early 12th century, the church was rebuilt in the 14th century by Richard "Dick" Whittington, c1358-1423, and who, according to Stow "was in this church three times buried, first by his executors . . . then in the reign of Edward the Sixth the Parson of the Church thinking that some great riches could be buried with him, caused his monument to be broken, and in the reign of Queen Mary, the Parishioners were forced to take him up and "lap him in lead as afore to bury him the third time". The church was destroyed in the Great Fire of 1666, after which time it was rebuilt by Wren. It suffered once again in 1944, this time as a result of a flying-bomb, and has since been well restored. One of the parish's illustrious 'men of the past' was Geoffrey Chaucer, who was born in Vintry Ward in 1310- "the son of a Vintner".

In his autobiography Thomas Mountague, rector here in the 16th century, recalls how he continued to read the service from the Book of Common Prayer of Edward VI, and to which the Queen, Mary I, strongly objected. He wrote "The next Sundaye after (the Coronation of Q. Mary—1689) Thomas Montagu, parson of Sent Myhellus in the towere ryall, otherwise callyd Tythtyngeton College—dyd ther mynystere al kyend of servys accordyngs to the godly order than sett forthe by that moste grasyus and blessye prence Kynge Edward the syxte". When in the 14th century rent was due to St. Katherine's Hospital, near the Tower of London, the Master of the Hospital would come to St. Michael's church to collect it from the Lord of the Manor of Reynham, in Kent, the records do not show why this custom should occur here—but it did. In the 16th century the rectors were also the master of the nearby College of Priests that had been set up by Dick Whittington in College Hill. The Master in 1537, one Richard Smith, was a prominent Catholic during the reign of Edward VI, and was obliged to retire in favour of Peter Martyr, but on the restoration of the Catholic Faith under Mary I, was reinstated both to his mastership here, as well as to his professorship at an Oxford college, in addition to which he was made a chaplain to the Queen. When Elizabeth I came to the throne in 1558, he once again, lost all his preferments and is later recorded as being 'well-received at Douai College', after which he is lost in the oblivion of time. From the church it is a short walk to **London Bridge** (16), the present structure having been built between 1967 and 1972, to the cost of £5.5 million. It is the fourth bridge in the near vicinity to the present day one. Cross over the bridge to the 'south' side of the River Thames, walk down the steps that lead to **Southwark (Anglican) Cathedral of St. Saviour** (17). After over five hundred years serving London as an Augustinian Priory St. Mary Overie surrendered in 1540 to the 'forces of the King'— Henry VIII, 1491-1547, at the time of the Dissolution of the Monasteries. At which time the parishioners of Southwark—the south ward of the City having been claimed by London in 1550 by the then Lord Mayor of London, Sir Rowland Hill 1549-1550—bought the church for the sum of £800. It was from this time that the name of the church became S. Saviour's. With the church being too large for the congregation they proceeded to wall up those portions for which they did not have any immediate use. This included the whole of the nave, and the area behind the High Altar—the retro-choir, the latter being let out, much to the disapproval of John Stow, 1525-1605, to a baker where he was allowed to set up his ovens, knead and bake dough. It was during the early 17th century that the nave became a stone quarry when much of the material was removed and used for other purposes. In the late 19th century the nave was once again rebuilt to the designs of Sir Arthur Blomfield, 1829-1899, in which he restored the tomb of Sir John Gower, 1330-1408, friend of Geoffrey Chaucer, is known as the "first English poet" being the first to write in English. His tomb can be seen in the north wall of the nave. Today the building offers the visitor a mixture of medieval and neo-gothic architecture of the 19th century.

It was to the or Borough of Southwark that Catholic martyrs were brought in the 16th and 17th centuries, there being no less than five prisons here at that time.

St. Margaret's Court in the Borough High Street marks the spot where the Parish Church of St. Margaret once stood, until it was pulled down in the 16th century when the parish was merged with the 'new' combined parish of S. Saviour's. Nearby was the Borough Compter, or prison, where a number of religious persons were held pending their trial, and in most cases death. Here, in 1539 were brought the Ven. John Griffith a priest and sometime vicar of Wandsworth (then in Surrey) and Dolton in Devon, and the Ven. John Waire, a Franciscan priest—both were hanged, drawn and quartered in Southwark on 8th July 1539. Two years later Blessed David Gonson, a layman and a Knight of St. John was executed here, and in 1600, Blessed John Rigby, another layman hung, drawn and quartered in Southwark, while in 1601 a seminary priest, Blessed John Pibush (was also hung, drawn and quartered) after having spent nearly twelve years in prison.

Return to London Bridge, and, on reaching the "North Bank" leave by way of the stairs on the right hand side of the bridge just past Adelaide House and so reach Lower Thames Street.

Here is the Parish Church of **St. Magnus the Martyr** (18), dedicated to St. Magnus of Orkney, murdered by his cousin in 1116 in a fit of jealousy and buried in Kirkwall Cathedral that is dedicated to him. Some doubt, however, has been expressed that the murder was not a justification for the martyrdom crown, and that the church was, originally, dedicated to one or other of the other martyrs named Magnus. Included in the 'also rans' is St. Magnus who "suffered in Caesarea in Cappadocia in the time of Aurelian the Emperor, Anno Dom. 276 under Alexander the governor", in which case the church's foundation can, justly, be claimed as being prior to 1328 when we read that Robert of St. Albans was appointed Rector of the church. Its place in medieval London, i.e. Catholic London, was quite considerable, at the close of the 16th century there were over one hundred parish churches in the City of London, or close by to it. Certainly it attracted to it some of the best known persons of the time. The English translator of the Bible, Miles Coverdale, 1488-1568, was rector of the church, later becoming the Bishop of Exeter—he left this country when Mary I, came to the Throne. In Switzerland he worked on the Geneva Bible (1557-1579). On his return he did not resume his work in Exeter, but carried out an extensive preaching mission throughout the country. On his death in 1568 he was first buried in the Parish Church of St. Bartholomew by the Exchange, and when that building was demolished in 1841, his body was transferred to St. Magnus the Martyr. The parish today represents the High Church (Anglo-Catholic) section of the Church of England, and as such keeps alive the memory of the Fraternity of Salve Regina which was founded here in 1343. Here in the middle ages was placed an image of the Salutation of the Virgin by the angel, and subscriptions from the members were devoted towards the five candles that were burned before it during the singing of the hymn, as well as for the maintenance of the chapel and its accessories. Buried in this chapel is Henry Yevele, c1320-1400, the

architect of Westminster Hall, and once described as the "Wren of
the 14th century", a member of the Fraternity who left money in his
will for a candle to burn perpetually before the image of Our Lady.
Also in the will of Nicholas Charleton, a Skinner by trade who died
in 1439, was left one hundred pounds of pure beeswax "to minister
and serve to the use of the Salve of Our Lady Chapel" in the church
of St. Augustine, Watling Street, close by St. Paul's Cathedral
where a branch of the Fraternity had been formed.

By a decree of Pope Innocent IV, in 1250 a bishop visiting his
diocese was permitted to summon all his clergy to one place for a
general meeting. From the 15th to the 17th century St. Magnus the
Martyr was chosen by the Bishop of London for this purpose. The
church was probably selected for its proximity to the river and the
nearby landing stages of Billingsgate and Swan Wharf. There are
two stories from the 16th century that are worth recording concern-
ing the parish at that time—the first being that between 1512 and
1527, the rector was one Geoffrey Wrenne, a forbear of Sir
Christopher Wren who was to rebuild the church after the Great
Fire of London in 1666. Geoffrey went on to become a Canon of
Windsor and lies buried in the north aisle of the chapel. The second
story warns of careless talk in the same century and the cost of a
loose tongue. In 1555 Julius III, 1487-1555, died and Stephen
Gardiner, who had followed Cardinal Wolsey as Bishop of
Winchester in 1531, wrote to the Bishop of London, Edmund
Bonner, ordering in Queen Mary's name a certain ceremony to be
conducted which is appointed by the Church of Rome during the
vacancy of the papal chair while a new Pope is being elected. A
notice was placed on the door of St. Magnus the Martyr, and on
asking a passer-by what it said, was told that the Pope was dead and
that she must pray for him. She refused to agree, and her refusal
came to the notice of the church, and she was placed in a cage on
London Bridge for several days and told to "cool herself". Early records of the church show its title as being "S. Magnus ad pontem",
"Saint Magnus on the bridge", and this gave rise to the rector making claims on the offerings that were made in the Chapel of St.
Thomas Becket that stood in the middle of the old London Bridge—
a parish boundary mark still shows the extent of the parish today on
the modern bridge. The dispute was finally settled and the parish
thereafter received the sum of twenty pence per year. At the begin-

ning of the reign of Elizabeth I, 1533-1603, there was an increase in the Protestant zeal, and Strype, 1643-1737, the successor of John Stow as London's leading historian, recalls "On Sep. 16 at St. Magnus at the corner of Fish Street, the Rood and Mary and John were burnt". The entry was dated 1559.

Continue to walk alongside the right hand side of the church on leaving the churchyard, noting en route the two sets of stones from two London Bridges near to the tower of the church.

From the 14th century the Corporation of the City of London was authorised by various Acts of Parliament to collect rents and tolls at **Billingsgate** (19), and to operate a free and open market for the wholesale sale of all fish here on this site. In 1981 the market was moved to a new site at West India Docks, and was formally opened by the Lord Mayor of London, Sir Anthony Jolliffe, G.B.E., on the 16th February 1982. Today the site is being redeveloped. Here in 1585 William Fleetwood, Recorder of the City of London, (1571), discovered a School for Pickpockets, and took the necessary action to close it down. Fleetwood was better known in 16th century London as being a "hunter of Papists".

Continue along Lower Thames Street until the **Custom House** is reached (20), rebuilt in 1821 by Sir Robert Smirke, 1781-1867, with a river frontage and riverside parade, alas not open to the public. However, a good view of both the river and the banks on either side can be seen by walking down the roadway at the side of the Custom House. Across the roadway from the House is the former parish church of **St. Dunstan in the East** (21). Now a 'restored' ruin, and made into a very pleasant garden in which to rest awhile on the walk. Founded in the 13th century, with a list of rectors going back to 1310, when John de Pretelwelle was first appointed, the church was badly damaged in the Great Fire of 1666, and repaired by Wren. In 1817-1821 the church, but not the tower and spire, was rebuilt by David Laing, 1774-1856. The church was gutted in the Second World War, 1939-1945, and, since 1971, has been an open-space in the City. Several people of interest have been associated with the church and including John Morton, rector between 1472-1474, later Bishop of Ely, and finally Archbishop of Canterbury and Lord Chancellor of England. By order of Henry VIII, the Court of Aldermen of the City were to assemble here at 7 a.m. on 8th February in 1540 "in the morning in their best clothes on their way to meet the Royal Party at

Greenwich". From the Churchwardens' Accounts, which date from 1450, it would appear that the parish owned "The Maid" in Tower Street, and that a quit rent was paid for it each year. In 1494's accounts there appears an item relating to "The Maid" viz. "Itm. Paid the 26th day of March Anno 1494. I departed with Master Parson to Canterbury to speak with my Lord Chancellor (John Morton who had been rector of the parish) for the church matter for the quit rent of x marks for the Maide in Tower Street, and the first day of April I came home to London again-the space of seven days spent I and my man with our two horses and horse hire. sum 10 shillings and 7½ pence". Another entry shows that two-pence was spent "On Corpus Christi day for bread and ale", and five pence on Easter Eve for a quarter of coals for the holy fire. A bottle of wine on Whitsunday was charged at sixpence, and there are many other items of interest in the accounts that relate to the running costs of churches in medieval, Pre-Reformation days, The Baptism Registers are also full of interest and show among other items that any foundlings baptised in the church were given the surname of either East Donstan, or East Dunstan. In the reign of Edward III, 1327-1377, a deserted child found in Sevenoaks, Kent was brought to London and baptised here in St. Dunstan's. He was apprenticed and admitted to the Worshipful Company of Grocers and as William Sevenoke, became the Lord Mayor of London 1418, and a Member of Parliament. He gave to Sevenoaks a Free School and Hospital. When he died he was buried in St. Martin Ludgate church (qv), and left them in his will of 1426 the sum of ten marks a year. The parish suffered its share of martyrs of the 16th century we read in Foxe's Book of Martyrs "On the 17th September 1557 four persons were burnt at Islington—namely Ralph Allerton, James Austoo, Margery Austoo and Richard Roth". All were condemned for heresy. Later in the same century at a meeting of the vestry on 27th December 1560 they were told in a letter from the Archbishop of Canterbury, Matthew Parker, that they had to remove the rood screen from the church in accordance with a general order for their removal from all churches at that time. Time, and weather permitting, it would seem most appropriate to rest here a short while and remember those parishioners of the 16th century who had to comply with orders that went against their upbringing and the traditions of the church from 'time out of memory' as John Stow was apt to say.

Walk up St. Dunstan's Hill, turn right at Great Tower Street and walk along until the **Parish Church of All Hallows** is reached (22). Of all the churches along this route about which one could say "If only the stones could speak" surely All Hallows by the Tower, or All Hallows Barkingchurche, must be the one which would be able to tell the most. Within these sacred walls have come over the past nine hundred years kings and queens, bishops and priests, saints and sinners, the high and mighty as well as the lowly both in heart and in estate. At some time they have all been here some have been alive on arrival others have been dead. Some died naturally and others were put to death either for their political or religious beliefs or even because they deserved it by the chosen way of living by theft, murder or plain intrigue. All have come, and some have gone from the church of All Hallows (All Saints) near to the Her Majesty's Royal Palace and Fortress of the Tower of London.

The finding after the bombing of the Second World War, 1939-1945, of a 7th century archway, that can still be seen under the 17th century tower, has settled, once and for all, the early foundation date for the church. It is believed to have been founded by St. Erkenwald, Bishop of London, 675-685. He also founded the monastic establishment at Barking, and gave them the parish which they provided the staff until the Dissolution of the Monasteries in the 16th century. During his reign Edward I, 1272-1307, presented to the church a statue of Our Lady of Barking, for a chapel in her honour. Later, in the time of Edward IV's reign, 1461-1470, and 1471-1483, a Brotherhood was established here in honour of Our Lady. But the chapel was destroyed in 1548, and the site used for secular purposes. Being situated so close to Tower Hill, a favourite execution place from early times until the 18th century, the church was often used as a temporary place of burial for those executed on The Hill. Here in 1535 came the body of Saint John Fisher, and in 1645 Archbishop William Laud, 1573-1645, the Anglican martyr beheaded on Tower Hill, for his support of Charles I, 1600-1649, against the Puritans. He was accused at his trial of being a "Papist" having used incence and a Latin form of service to dedicate St. Katharine Creechurch. The church is built over the site of a Roman villa, a pavement from which can be seen in the crypt of the church. In the crypt chapel are the ashes of a number of members of Toc H, whose church this is, including those of its founder "Tubby" Clayton.

Finally we cross the roadway at the end east of the church to walk to **Tower Hill Gardens** (23).

Here, took place hundreds of executions over a period of three hundred years. Of the Catholic martyrs that suffered death here the first was Simon of Sudbury, Archbishop of Canterbury, 1375-1381, who was dragged from the Tower of London by the followers of Wat Tyler in 1381 and crudely beheaded on the Hill. His head and that of Robert Hales were then paraded around the City on stakes and deposited on the gate of London Bridge—from where Simon's head was rescued and can now be seen in a special, glazed, cupboard in the vestry of St. Gregory's church in Sudbury, Suffolk. The archbishop's body was returned to Canterbury where it lies in the cathedral. On 22nd June 1535 Saint John Fisher, Cardinal and Bishop of Rochester was taken from the Tower of London and beheaded for "treason"; he was followed, on 6th July 1535 by Saint Thomas More, a layman, Lord Chancellor of England "The King's good servant, but God's first". Both their heads were displayed on London Bridge, and both their bodies were interred in the Church of St. Peter ad Vincula in the **Tower of London** (24). In recent years a small shrine has been permitted in the undercroft of the church in memory of Saint Thomas More, whose head was rescued, by his daughter Margaret Roper. It was buried with her in the Anglican Parish Church of St. Dunstan outside the West Gate of the City of Canterbury. On his canonisation in 1935, the Anglican authorities permitted a marble stone to be placed over the vault in the church recording the life and death of the saint. In the following year to Fisher and More's death, 1539, Blessed Adrian Fortescue and the Venerable Thomas Dingley were both beheaded on Tower Hill. The last Catholic martyr, but by no means the last person to be beheaded on Tower Hill was Blessed William Howard, who was the grandson of Saint Philip Howard, who lies enshrined in the Catholic Cathedral at Arundel, West Sussex. He was also beheaded, having been condemned for being involved in "the Plot", on the 29th December 1680.

It has been said that there can be hardly a sadder or a bloodier spot in London than on Tower Hill all those years ago, and yet the records show that people flocked to see the executions by their thousands. So many people were expected on some occasions that special stands were erected for their "comfort".

St Benet's Paul's Wharf

Her Majesty's Royal Palace and Fortress

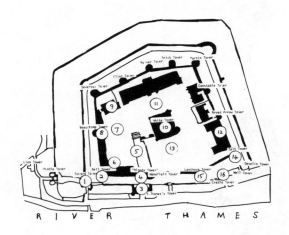

1 Byward Tower
2 Bell Tower
3 St.Thomas's Tower
4 "Bloody Tower"
5 Archway
6 Queen's House
7 Execution block site
8 Beauchamp Tower
9 St.Peter Ad Vincula
10 White Tower
11 Parade Ground
12 New Armouries
13 Royal Palace, site of
14 Salt Tower
15 Lanthorn Tower
16 Cradle Tower

Her Majesty's Royal Palace and Fortress

Ever since William the Conqueror ordered the building of the White Tower on the edge of London's city wall it has attracted visitors.

Technically, the Tower is a concentric castle which stands on the north bank of the River Thames on the eastern side of the City of London. Including the moat, now dry, and Tower Wharf, now a popular promenade, the ground covers 18 acres, the area within the outer wall of the castle being approximately 12 acres. Dominating the whole castle complex is the White Tower which was built within the southeast corner of the City Wall. The architect was Gundulph, Bishop of Rochester, 1024-1108. He rebuilt much of his own cathedral, and a nunnery at West Malling. The existing curtain walls were built during the period between 1189 and 1306, with the majority of the work being completed during the reign of Henry III, 1261-1272; The Wakefield Tower and the water-gatehouse, called St. Thomas's Tower, or more popularly 'Traitors' Gate', and certain other features date from Henry III's time. Today's Tower of London reflects the restoration work carried out by Anthony Salvin, 1799-1881, an authority on medieval strongholds, who was able to correct the many mistakes of earlier restorers. Although many of its visitors concentrate on its history as a prison and place of torture, it has been many things besides being a place of imprisonment. A royal palace, and a court of justice were held in the Tower, with the quarter sessions being removed by James I, 1566-1625, but in later times a Court of Requests were held in Stepney, with a Steward appointed by the Constable of the Tower of London, which dealt with offences of debt, trespass, and covenants in the Liberties. The

Liberties were those places that did not come within the jurisdiction of the Lord Mayor of London, and consisted mainly of areas around the larger religious houses that could, and did, claim sanctuary for criminals. The last of these areas to succumb to the Crown was the Little and Great Sanctuary of Westminster Abbey where the Dean, the successor to the Abbot, held out until the 17th century. From their palace in the Tower, a series of buildings in front of the White Tower which were demolished during the Commonwealth period of the 17th century, sovereigns went in stately procession to Westminster for their Coronations at Westminster Abbey. Charles II, 1630-1685, was the last to make the customary procession. In addition to the Tower being a fortress it had also been a naval depot and the workshop of the Crown. Off Tower Wharf the king's ships were moored, while their stores and equipment were housed in the Tower. Records show that the *Nicholas*, and other "Ships of the Tower", as they were called, were refitted and "stored up" here in readiness to put to sea as fighting members of the Royal Navy. Today the Tower Wharf is a museum of guns of various periods and nationalities. Here the Honourable Artillery Company, (HAC), the Lord Mayor of London's personal bodyguard, fires salutes on the anniversaries of the birth, accession, and coronation of the monarch, and on certain other occasions during the course of the year. For centuries the Tower was a munitions factory, from it came the longbows for Crecy and for Agincourt, here too the Tower guns were made and repaired. In Stuart times, hundreds of barrels of gunpowder were stored in the White Tower. When the Great Fire of London of 1666 was raging the King, Charles II, and the diarists Pepys and Evelyn were deeply concerned about the gunpowder in the Tower. Fortunately the wind changed and instead of moving towards the Tower it blew away into the heart of the City. In later times the magazine was removed to Hyde Park. In the Tower was *the* Wardrobe, the accounting, purchasing and stores department of the Crown, it kept the costs of war, supplied armour and clothing the weapons and missiles to the troops. Also here was the Ordnance, an early Ministry of Munitions, which was taken over by the War Office in 1855, but an offspring from it, the Ordnance Survey, now at Southampton, had its early O.S. maps inscribed "Engraved in the Drawing Room in the Tower of London". The Tower Officers of the Ordnance began the survey of Britain. *The* Mint was in the Tower, as was a money exchange where anybody could bring their gold and silver and have it converted into the coins of the Realm. There was also a Treasury in the Tower where the bankers of the City of London brought their cash and other valuables for safe keeping. Treasures brought home by Sir Walter Raleigh after he had circumnavigated the world were stored for a time in the vaults. The first public library was once to be found in the Wakefield Tower, made up mainly of the State Archives, all neatly indexed and made available for Tudor and later antiquarians. In the 18th century a yearly ticket cost ten shillings and sixpence, and the library was open from 8 am until 12 noon in the morning, and from 2 p.m to 6 p.m in the afternoon.

Today among the many thousands of visitors to the Tower of London there are those who visit it as pilgrims of Faith to find the sites where the martyrs of the English Reformation were imprisoned, tortured and in most cases died proclaiming Jesus Christ as their Lord and Master.

The entrance to the Tower of London today is by way of the lower portion of Tower Hill, and, passes over the ruins of the Lion Tower, where once was the Royal Menagerie that housed various wild animals that had been given to the kings. Shortly there can be seen the Middle Tower, where tickets are checked and any security precautions taken. Once under the archway of the tower, and passing over a short causeway over the now dry moat, the **Byward Tower** (1) built in 1280 can be found. Here the nightly "Ceremony of the Keys" takes place just before 10 o'clock. The Tower is locked up for the night and after that time any of the inhabitants of the Tower wishing to gain entrance must identify themselves before being allowed inside the gatehouse. A by-word (password) is also needed in the latter part of the night watch, hence the Byward Tower's name, to admit persons staying out late into the night. This ceremony has continued for at least nine hundred years, if not longer. Tickets are issued to members of the public who wish to witness this most ancient of ceremony, but they should be applied for well in advance as there are only a limited number available each night.

Immediately after entering the Outer Ward, walking along Water Lane, the **Bell Tower** (2) can be seen. This tower is one of the oldest and was erected in the late 12th and early 13th centuries. One of the curfew towers of the City of London, its bell would ring out over the city to tell its inhabitants to *"cover the fire and prepare for the night"*, and would ring out each morning to awaken the population from its sleep and to start another day's work. The word is from the Old French, *couvrefeu*, which literally means *"cover-fire"*. William the Conqueror instituted the Curfew in this country, and set the time at 8 o'clock each evening in 1068. Today the word is used by occupying armies as being the time when all civilians must be indoors or suffer punishment for being "abroad after Curfew".

The ringing of the bell was also the sign for prisoners' visitors and other non-residents of the Tower to leave—at the present time it still denotes that the visiting hours for the day are over. The present bell was cast in 1615 and it is the only curfew bell in regular use in London today. The only way into the tower has always been, through the Queen's House for the lower floor where Saint Thomas More was imprisoned, and by way of the battlement from the Beauchamp Tower for the upper floor, known also as the "strong-room". It was in the latter room that Saint John Fisher, Bishop of Rochester from 1504 until his execution in 1535, was imprisoned. Both of these saints were imprisoned for their Faith refuseing to support Henry VIII, 1491-1547, in his decision to reject the religious laws of Pope, Clement VII, revoking his marriage to Katharine of Aragon, to marry Anne Boleyn. Many of More's visitors tried in vain to persuade him to change his views, so that he could be allowed to return to his family. He refused to be moved from the Truth, and although complaining about the conditions under which he was kept, deprived of food, clothing and bedding, writing materials, he was steadfast in his resolve. At the same time that More was in the lower room John Fisher was being kept in solitary confinement in the upper room. He too found guilty of treason for refusing to accept the king's royal supremacy and for not accepting the king's "right" to divorce Katharine. In a letter to Thomas Cromwell, c.1485-1540, the English statesman who was responsible for carrying out Henry VIII's Reformation, Fisher writes begging for some relief in his situation. He complains that his clothes are in rags, asks for food that he could digest and some books to comfort him. His request for a confessor was granted, but at the same time Master Rich, later Lord Rich, and newly appointed as the King's Solicitor, was sent "to confer" with each of the confessors in a vain attempt to trap them into admitting under the disguise of a friendly conversation, statements that could be used against More and Fisher at their trials for treason against the State. Both men stood firm to the end in the verity of their beliefs were beheaded on Tower Hill in 1535. After their deaths their headless bodies, (the heads being displayed on the city gate,) were brought back into the Tower and buried in the Chapel Royal of St. Peter ad Vincula, the parish church of the Tower of London.

Walk along Water Lane towards **Traitors's Gate** (3), which is one of the most famous spots of English history. More correctly called St. Thomas's Tower and Water Gate, it was erected during the reign of Henry III, 1216-1272, the cost of the building was borne by the citizens of London, and was not popular, as their taxes were increased as a result. Originally the king only intended to make a watergate entrance to the Tower, but, realising that it presented a breach in the defences had the tower attached to it as an afterthought. Tradition tells that the arch, sixty one feet across, twice fell down, and that on the last occasion one of the guards saw a ghostly figure, dressed in bishops' clothing, knocking down the arch. When challenged by the guard the figure acknowledged that he was Thomas of Canterbury and that *"we mislikes these works because they are raised in scorn, and against the public right"*. The king was quick to take up the point and dedicated the oratory in the tower to the archbishop, whereupon the work continued unhampered, and the archway remains intact.

Although no longer filled with the water from the Thames, it still stands sentinel over both river and castle. It should be noted that the archway has no keystone each stone of the lowest course is keyed into the next one by a cog, for which there has been a space cut for it in the adjoining stone. It was not until the 16th century that the archway became the recognised landing-place for any prisoners brought down from trial at Westminster Hall, then the official Royal Courts of Justice, and it is from those days that it acquired its popular name of "Traitors's Gate". After his examination at Lambeth Palace by the Archbishop of Canterbury, Thomas Cranmer, 1489-1556, the Lord Chancellor, Secretary Cromwell, and Saint Thomas More landed here at the entrance to the Tower. On his arrival the porter demanded, as was his right and privilege, his top coat, but Thomas More gave him instead his hat. Whereupon the porter replied *"No, sir, I must have your gown"*, which was duly handed over to him by the saint. After his trial, at which he was found guilty of *"traitorously attempting to deprive the King of his title of Supreme Head of the Church"*, Thomas More took his last long farewell of his eldest daughter, Margaret Roper on the steps that lead down to the riverside. Today the tower is the residence of the Keeper of the Jewel House. Opposite Traitors's Gate is the **"Bloody Tower"** (4), or, again, more correctly the Garden Tower. Since the brutal murder here of the "Two young Princes in the tower", Edward V, 1470-1483, and his younger brother Richard of York, in 1483 the tower has been referred to by its more popular title. Entrance to the tower is by way of the **steps** (5) on the left hand side of the walkway just after passing under the archway. They lead immediately to the green in front of the **Queen's House** (6), turn left at the top of the steps and walk to the rampart known as Raleigh's Walk. Here is the upper entrance to the Bloody Tower. It is also suggested that the tower acquired this name after the death of Percy, 8th Earl of Northumberland in 1585. Although a loyal supporter of Elizabeth I, he gathered forces together after the Rebellion of the Northern Earls in 1569, and later became connected with a group of men that included the Duke of Guise and Cardinal Allen, forcing the Queen to release Mary Queen of Scots. Detained in the Tower for a year without trial, the Lieutenant was ordered to change his jailer who was replaced by a servant of Sir Christopher Hatton, the Lord Chancellor and a favourite of the Queen. The next morning the Earl was found dead by the servant, and although a verdict of suicide was recorded by the coroner, it was assumed that he killed himself rather than face the confiscation of his estates should he have been brought to trial under the Bill of Attainder and found guilty.

Earlier in the 16th century the tower was also used to imprison the Archbishop of Canterbury, Thomas Cranmer, Bishop Hugh Latimer of Worcester, and Bishop Nicholas Ridley of Rochester. All three were transported from the Tower of London by barge to Oxford, where they were burnt alive. Ridley and Latimer on the 16th October 1555, and the archbishop on 21st March 1556. A monument in St. Giles's Street, Oxford, known as the Martyrs' Memorial, was erected in 1841, to the designs of Sir Gilbert Scott, with sculptures by Henry Weekes, 1807-1877, of the three martyrs. For their implication in the "Gunpowder Plot" two Jesuit priests were incarcerated here in 1605. Father Garnot SJ, was hanged in St. Paul's

Churchyard on the 3rd May 1606, and Father Oldcorn was taken to Worcester and there was hanged, cut down while still alive, disembowelled and quartered. William Laud, 1573-1645, and the Archbishop of Canterbury from 1633 until his execution in 1645, was kept captive here after his stand against the Puritans. He supported Charles I, 1600-1649, who himself was to die a martyr's death in 1649 at the hands of Oliver Cromwell, 1599-1658, as well as the ill-fated Thomas Wentworth, Earl of Stafford, who was beheaded on Tower Hill in May 1641 *"before a vast crowd"*. Laud demanded religious uniformity based on the views of the High Anglican movement, and in order to subdue opponents he used the Star Chamber a medieval court of justice which was composed of the King's Council, suitably reinforced with judges. It met in the Star Chamber of the old Palace of Westminster, whose ceiling was painted with stars. It earnt itself a reputation for hardness of judgements. At his trial Laud was accused of "popish practices" such as the use of incense and Latin during Divine Services, and in 1630, as the Bishop of London, he consecrated St. Katharine Creechurch in the City of London. He was condemned to death and was beheaded on Tower Hill in 1645. At first buried in the nearby Parish Church of All Hallows by the Tower, his body was later removed and re-interred in the chapel of St. John's College Oxford, where in 1630 the second quadrangle for his old college was begun. It is now known as the Canterbury Quadrangle.

From the Bloody Tower it is a short walk to **Tower Green** (7) and the place of executions which took place within the walled area of the Tower of London. The paved area in front of the Parish Church of St. Peter ad Vincula was used for "private" executions, and although today the area may seem to the visitor to be inconspicuous, on days of executions a five foot high scaffold would be erected and draped in black. Executions here were rare but among the six recorded names that of Margaret, Countess of Salisbury, mother of Cardinal Reginald Pole, Archbishop of Canterbury from 1556 to 1558, whose "crimes" were thus being the mother of the Archbishop, and a Plantagenet, deemed to have had designs on the Throne of England. She was beheaded without trial or without even the formulation of charges against her.

To the left of the scaffold site is the **Beauchamp Tower** (8), built about 1300, which takes its name from Thomas Beauchamp, Earl of

Warwick, imprisoned here from 1397-1399. He was one of the "Lord Appellant", who rebelled against the government of Richard II, 1366-1399, and was executed for his part in the plot.

The most interesting feature of the tower is the inscriptions, over ninety in all made, by the prisoners themselves. Only the second floor is now open to the public, the upper floors being the residence of one of the Yeomen Warders of the Tower of London. Here can be seen some of the most interesting of the inscriptions. They do not all occupy their original positions in the building, having been rearranged for the benefit of visitors. Above the fireplace is to be found inscription number 13. This inscription was cut by Saint Philip Howard, Earl of Arundel and Surrey, in Latin, which translated read *"The more affliction we endure for Christ in this world, the more glory we shall obtain with Christ in the next"*. He was accused and found guilty, of being reconciled to the "old faith", and was imprisoned here from 1585 until he died in 1595. He died on Sunday, 19th October 1595 and was buried next to his father in a plain coffin, in the Chapel of St. Peter ad Vincula. In 1624 his widow, Anne, and their son, obtained permission from James I, 1566-1625, to remove his body to the Fitzalan Church of Arundel Castle, and to place it in the vault there for safe keeping. In 1929 Pope Pius XI, 1857-1939, pronounced his beatification, and then, forty years on, in October 1970, together with thirty-nine other English and Welsh martyrs, he was canonised by Pope Paul VI, 1897-1978. In the following year Saint Philip Howard's remains were solemnly transferred from the vault in the castle to a new shrine in the north transept of Arundel Cathedral, Sussex. Inscription number 66 belongs to Thomas Abel, and takes the form of a *rebus* with a large "A" on a bell under the word Thomas. He was the domestic chaplain to Queen Katharine of Aragon, 1485-1536, and a fearless critic of Henry VIII's divorce proceedings .He was executed at Smithfield in July 1540.

Also of great interest is number 19 "Ihon Store, Doctor, 1570", his first "crime" against the State was in 1549 when he opposed the original Act of Uniformity, which imposed the exclusive use of the Book of Common Prayer in all public services and laid down heavy penalties for those who failed to comply. There are many other inscriptions that are worth looking for including numbers 20, Charles Bailly, courier to Mary Queen of Scots, and numbers 33, 47, 52 and 57 which commemorate members of the Pole family. Number 81 has an inscription *"En Dieu est mon esperance"*, that is, *"In God is my hope"* and bears the name Page. The Ven. Francis Page, a Jesuit priest was executed at Tyburn in 1602. In the previous year, 1601, St. Anne Line had been arrested and hung for harbouring Francis Page at her house in Holborn.

The **Chapel Royal of St. Peter ad Vincula** (9), the Parish Church of the Tower of London, as opposed to the Chapel of St. John in the White Tower, is not freely available to visitors, unless they have come to attend a service. Normally the only way to obtain entrance to the church, is by being part of an official party conducted by the Yeoman Warders of the Tower. Every effort should be made to visit the chapel under one or other of these auspices. Here the majority of the people who were beheaded on Tower Hill, were laid to rest Those beheaded on Tower Green were also buried here in the chapel, but there is nothing to suggest that their heads were taken outside the precincts of the Tower of London. If the distinguished men and women were buried amid the pomp and circumstance of their time in Westminster Abbey or St. Paul's Cathedral, here were buried the "failures". Without any kind of ceremony at all, no covering to their coffins on the last sad journey to the grave, frequently with no mark of identification left with the bodies on the stone slab above them. When Lord Macaulay, 1800-1859, the historian and statesman, wrote that there is no sadder spot on earth—he wrote the truth. In 1876 Queen Victoria, 1819-1901, visited the Tower. She complained about the condition of the chapel, and ordered that it should be restored and that *all* the graves should be identified and re-interred. After research the experts on restoration were able to conclude that under the altar were buried Queens Anne Boleyn and Katherine Howard, Jane Viscountess Rochford, Sir Allan Apsley, the Dukes of Somerset and of Northumberland, and Margaret Pole, Countess of Salisbury. At the same time the area around the altar was re-tiled with the coat of arms of those buried there. Within the chapel also lies buried William Howard (Viscount Stafford), John Fisher and Saint Thomas More. The latter now has a shrine dedicated in 1970 in the crypt of the chapel, used by pilgrims for their private prayers. Here is also to be found a bust of St. Thomas More, by Raphael Maklouf.

Standing 92 feet high in the centre of the enclosed area is the **White Tower**, (10) the original building of the Tower of London. Today the entrance to the tower is by way of the wooden staircase on the south (river) side of the building. Rising four storeys in height the tower houses many items of historical interest, including one of the finest collections of armour to be found anywhere in the world. The Tower's top floor was reserved for the Royal family and the Court, the third for nobility, the second for the chapel, with the retainers (servants) and the soldiers using the first floor, by which the public enter the Tower today. The basement was used for the storing of food and arms, and later for torturing prisoners. Except for a few hours during the 1381 Wat Tyler Rebellion, the White Tower has never been subjected to direct land attack. In one corner of the basement, close by the sub crypt of St. John's Chapel there is to be found a round headed doorway this is the only cell in the Tower, there being no *"dark, deep dungeons, nor could the basements be flooded by a rising Thames"*. Barely larger than a household cupboard, it measures 10 feet by 8 feet. According to tradition Sir Walter Raleigh was once imprisoned here, and the inscriptions on the shows evidence that Messrs Robert Rudston, Thomas Fane, and Thomas Culpeper were imprisoned here for their part in the Thomas Wyatt rebellion. They were conspirators in a plot to prevent Mary I, 1516-1558, from marrying Philip II of Spain, 1527-1598, that was led by Sir Thomas Wyatt, c.1521-1554, who marched on London from Kent. They failed to capture the Capital, surrendered and were executed. Wyatt himself, after a short stay in the Tower of London, was found guilty of treason and beheaded on Tower Hill. Find and walk up the 13th century spiral staircase that leads to the Chapel of St. John the Evangelist, here in the peace and quiet pause and look carefully at the magnificent architecture of the chapel, one of the finest examples of Romanesque (Norman) architecture anywhere in the country. Built between 1080 and 1088, and described by one former Constable of the Tower as being "The Jewel of the Crown". Today's visitors see the chapel shorne of most of its former glory, Henry III, 1207-1272, gave instructions that it should be painted and fitted out with "arras and tapestries", it was not until the 19th century scoured and cleaned that the stonework was once more revealed. Up to the time of Elizabeth I this chapel was regularly used by members of the Royal Family. After Charles II's time it became a repository for State Papers and was not cleared of them until 1857 when they were removed to the newly built Public Records Office in Chancery Lane. The peace was thoroughly disturbed in 1381 when some of the mob that followed Wat Tyler forced their way into the chapel where the Archbishop of Canterbury, Simon of Sudbury, was praying before the altar. He and Sir Robert Hales, the Treasurer and another official were dragged out of the chapel, taken to Tower Hill and beheaded.

After his murder in the Wakefield Tower the body of Henry VI, 1421-1461, lay in state here.

In 1553 in this chapel Mary I went through a form of marriage to Philip, King of Spain the Count Egmont acted as proxy. In the same year, in a vain attempt to save his life, John Dudley, Duke of Northumberland denied most vehemently his adherence to the Protestant Faith of the previous reign of Edward VI, 1537-1553. But he, with two others, Sir John Gates and the Earl of Warwick, making the same claim were all executed on Tower Hill. The chapel has also seen debates of a different nature such as the occasion when Saint Edmund Campion, S.J. was arraigned in public debate with the Dean of Windsor, the Dean of St. Paul's, and other leading theologians, who were suitably supported with many books of reference to quote from during the discussions. However the Saint and his companion in the trial, Ralph Sherwin, had no such advantages as their opponents—having been brought into the chapel direct from the "Little Ease" in the basement of the Tower and having been broken and crippled on the rack. They were both found guilty, and, on the 1st December 1581, tied to a hurdle and dragged from the Tower of London to Tyburn where they were hung, drawn and quartered.

From the chapel the way leads through into the Sword Room with the adjoining Banqueting Room. It was in the former room that nominees for the Order of the Bath, Britain's second oldest Order of Chivalry, were ceremoniously washed the night before their investiture, and, having been signed "with the sign of the Cross" on their bare backs, were "wined and dined" in the Banqueting Room. Walking up the spiral staircase in the corner of the room the visitor arrives in the Council Chamber where the kings and queens of England have presided over meetings from the earliest of times. Here, in 1535, came the first of the Reformation martyrs the Carthusian priors and their companions. From London came St. John Houghton, from Axholme House, in Lincolnshire, St. Augustine

Webster, and from Beauvale, in Nottinghamshire came St. Robert
Lawrence, each in their turn denouncing Henry VIII by saying *"The
King, our sovereign lord, is not Supreme Head on earth of the Church
of England"*. They were sentenced to be hung, drawn and quartered,
on 4th May 1535 at Tyburn. From here walk *down* the spiral staircase to the basement of the White Tower. Here was the area of
detention for the prisoners. In the south east corner is the infamous
"Little Ease", a small room barely four feet square, in which a prisoner could neither sit or lie down. It is virtually built into the thick-
ness of the wall of the Tower. There was also "The Pit" a twenty foot
deep, dark dingy cavelike place of detention. Today the basement is
well lit and clean and many visitors are almost disappointed when
they see it. In the 16th century the instruments of torture that must
have put fear even into the strongest of hearts were also to be found
here. The principal devices were the rack, a series of wheels to
which were attached ropes or chains that were capable of pulling
various parts of the body in different directions at the same time,
and   "The   Scavenger's   Daughter",   invented   by   Sir   Leonard
Skeffington, the Lieutenant of the Tower in the reign of Henry VIII.
This was a combination that allowed the hands to be fixed into iron
gloves, the arms and legs to be manacled, with a spiked collar round
the neck. This permitted teeth to be extracted or broken, and the
rack applied without let or hindrance on the part of the victim. Torture was never legalised in this country, although it was authorised
in the Middle Ages in order to procure evidence, to extract confes-
sions and as an aid to religious persecution. When in the 14th century the Knights Templars were ordered by the King to be tortured,
nobody could be found who was a skilled torturer throughout the
kingdom. Father Gerard, SJ was first brought into the chamber and
advised that he would sample all the devices that he could see. He
was suspended by his wrists screwed into iron bands, so that his feet
did not touch the floor beneath him. He fainted three times and
three times he was revived by vinegar poured down his throat.
Finally the Lieutenant of the Tower intervened and he was released
and sent to the Cradle Tower, where we shall meet him once again
on the walk. It was also in one of the two "cells" that Saint John
Southwell, SJ was tortured. He was transferred to the Tower of
London, from the Gatehouse Westminster. In the Council Chamber, he was "examined" thirteen times tortured in the basement,

questioned again. At his trial John Southwell admitted that he had not been "put to the rack", but that he had suffered *"new tortures worse than the rack"*. Among other prisoners for their Faith in the 16th century were three priests, Fathers James Fenn, Thomas Hemmerford and John Nutter all of whom, after having received the sentence of death, were laid in the Pit and "loaded with iron" until they were taken from the Tower. In the same year, 1584, Father Robert Nutter was imprisoned in the Pit for over forty days, during which time he also was tortured on Scavenger's Daughter. When Father Alexander Briant was transferred here from another prison in London he was heavily shackled, and needles thrust under his nails, thrown into the Pit, and 'severely racked'. One of a shipment of over twenty priests to be transported to France and banished *"from this realm for ever"*, Father J. Hart entered into the Jesuit Order while imprisoned here. A man of distinguished academic learning he was at first kept in irons for twenty days because he would not yield to the minister Mr Reynolds.

On the way to the stairs that lead to the Parade Ground of the Tower of London look for the brass plaque which records an explosion set off by the Irish Republican Army (IRA) on 17th July 1974, which killed one person and injured thirty-five. On reaching the **Parade Ground** (11), turn to the right and follow the roadway round passing on the left the Hospital Block which housed prisoners of war during the Second World War for a short time. To the side of this block, standing detached from it, is the **New Armouries** (12), or "C" block as it was once called. Built sometime before 1685, it has over the ensuing years been used as a storage house for horse armour, an Army Ordnance Depot, and a barrack for military personnel. In 1947 it was given to the Master of the Armouries as an extension for his exhibition. Opposite this building, and with a few ruins showing above ground level, stood the former **Royal Palace** (13). This was destroyed during the time of the Commonwealth of the 17th century, and at a time when the country was being ruled by Oliver Cromwell.

In the south-east corner of the inner bailey wall, next to "C" Block, is the **Salt Tower** (14), and is one of the oldest towers of the whole network of defences that surround the White Tower. For greater security it was later attached to the outer wall by a short stretch of walling. The tower is three storeys high with a vaulted ground floor room, continuing a fine old fireplace and on the first floor rooms, mainly used to imprison Jesuits in the 16th and 17th centuries, with an extensive collection of inscriptions on its walls. Confined here, and accused of being a witch, Hugh Draper of Byrstow, inscribed an elaborate horoscope on the wall. *"Hew Draper of Byrstow made this sphere the 30 days of Maye anno 1561"*. At least six of the inscriptions are made up of the monogram I H S, which is derived from the first two and the last letter of the Greek spelling of Jesus Christ, and not as often erroneously supposed from the Latin *"Iesus Hominum Salvator"*, i.e. *"Jesus the Saviour of Mankind"*, and adopted by the Society of Jesus (SJ) as their own monogram. One of the names of the prisoners here that appears no less than three times is St. Henry Walpole SJ. He was condemned under the statutes of 1518 and 1585, and hung, drawn and quartered at York in 1595. During his trial he confirmed that he had been tortured fourteen times. This tower has so many associations with the Society of Jesus names like Francis Betty, J. Lyon, Christopher Perry, William May, Michael Moody, etc., will forever live in the hearts of the faithful. Father John Gerard, SJ, records how he prayed before the "oratory" that Father Walpole had carved on the wall of a room here. It was in this room that Jesuits, accused at the time of the infamous Gunpowder Plot of 1605, imprisoned St. Nicholas Owen, a Jesuit lay-brother, who died under torture, although it was announced that he had stabbed himself to death. But the death is recorded by the Lieutenant of the Tower of the time as *"the man is dead—he died in our hands"*, may, I suppose be taken which ever way the reader wishes. Father Garnet, SJ, was executed in St. Paul's Churchyard in May 1606, and Edward Oldcorne, after suffering on the rack no less than five times was sent to Worcester to be executed in April 1606.

From the Salt Tower down the roadway that leads to the inner bailey wall passing the **Lanthorn Tower** (15), on the right and walk through the archway which leads to the outer bailey and Water Lane once more, here is the **Cradle Tower** (16). Built in the 14th century, this gateway was used at a time when its more notorious neighbour, Traitors's Gate, was out of action but, by the kings and queens wishing to stay in the Royal Apartments here. Like the Salt Tower this tower has close associations with the Jesuits, but fortunately of the more pleasant kind. Here was imprisoned Francis Arden, one of the "Ardens of Warwickshire", whose family were to suffer much at the hand of the persecutors of the Faith in the 16th century. It is the same family to which Mary Arden, the mother of William Shakespeare belonged. At the same time Francis Arden was in the Cradle Tower, Father Gerard was confined to the Salt Tower and the two were able to exchange messages between the two towers. Mrs Arden, who was allowed to visit her husband from time to time, surreptitiously took in to him all that was needed for a celebration of the Mass. On the Feastday of Our Lady's birth, 8th September, the two prisoners were allowed to celebrate the feast together. Father Gerard consecrated twenty-two Hosts for his own use and took them back to the Salt Tower and secreted them in a recess in the chimney-breast. Later, when Father Gerard was transferred to the Cradle Tower, he was able from the roof of the tower, to communicate with his friends outside. In this way he was able to arrange his and Francis Arden's escape to the boat nearby in which two lay-brothers of the Jesuit Order were waiting to take them to safety. In spite of the fact that Father Gerard's hands had been badly treated in the tortures that he had had to endure he managed to crawl to the waiting boat. Before leaving the Cradle Tower Father Gerard wrote a letter to the Lieutenant of the Tower of London exonerating him and his warder from any blame for the escape. In fact he left a small annuity to the latter for *"his goodness and kindness"*.

From the Cradle Tower it is a short walk, along Water Lane, to Traitors' Gate, and the Byward Tower and returning, once more, to the hustle and bustle of the twentieth century.

St. Thomas's Tower
alias Traitors' Gate

City centre—"heart and pride"

1	Royal Exchange	14	St. Peter upon Cornhill
2	Bank of England	15	St. Michael upon Cornhill
3	Statue of Ariel	16	Pasqua Rosee
4	Statue of Sir John Soane	17	Pope's Head Alley
5	St. Margaret Lothbury	18	St. Mary Woolnoth
6	Drapers' Hall	19	Abchurch Lane
7	Austin Friars	20	St. Mary Abchurch
8	Stock Exchange	21	Cannon Street Station
9	Royal Exchange Buildings	22	London Stone
10	St. Anthony's Hospital	23	Walbrook
11	Merchant Taylors' Hall	24	St. Stephen Walbrook
12	St. Martin Outwich	25	Mansion House
13	Standard upon Cornhill	26	St. Mary Woolchurch Haw

City Centre—"heart and pride"

The area around the Bank of England has often been said to be the heart of the City of London. From here the great monetary decisions are taken that affect men and women not only of the United Kingdom but throughout the world.

Here too can be found reminders of the city of yesteryear. Here can be seen buildings far older than the Bank of England which was founded in the 17th century as a result of the need for money to finance a war against France.

Sheltering under the gaunt, modern, structures can be found many churches.

We start our journey from Bank underground station. The exit to find is the one that will lead to the Royal Exchange, (there are two, but they both will take the walker to the front of the **Royal Exchange** (1).)

Founded in 1566, by Sir Thomas Gresham, 1519-1579, the present building dates from 1844, its predecessor having been destroyed by fire in 1838. It was designed by Sir William Tite, 1798-1873. Originally built as an Exchange for merchants, it no longer performs this function. The perimeter of the building is taken up by offices and shops, the centre being occupied by the London International Financial Futures Exchange. Appropriately at the "hour of the Rosary", 9, 12, 3, and 6 the Carillon plays English, Scottish, Irish, Welsh, Canadian and Australian melodies. It is from the steps of the Exchange that Royal Proclamations are made such as when a sovereign dies and the name of his, or her, successor is made public. In front of the Exchange stands the memorial to the London soldiers who died in the two World Wars of this century it was designed by

Sir Aston Webb, 1849-1930, with the bronzes by Alfred Drury, 1857-1944.

Across the roadway is the **Bank of England** (2) which was founded in 1694 by Royal Charter in order to collect funds for the war against Louis XIV of France, 1638-1715. It has since become the "bankers' bank", and the banker to the Government. The present building was completed in 1939, to the designs of Sir Herbert Baker, 1862-1946, who retained in his plans the outer walls constructed by Sir John Soane, 1753-1837. After the "No Popery Riots" of the 18th century a nightly picquet was provided by the Brigade of Guards and continued until 1973 when it was stopped. In the central court-yard stands a bronze statue of the Bank's patron saint, St. Christopher, by Richard Reginald Goulden, 1877-1932, and is a memorial to the fifty-five members of the Bank's staff who lost their lives in the First World War, 1914-1918. In the entrance hall the mosaics were designed by Boris Anrep, who also was responsible for the decoration of the Blessed Sacrament Chapel in Westminster Cathedral. Unfortunately the Bank's regulations no longer allow public access to the hall. The doors were the work of Charles Wheeler, 1892-1974, who was also responsible for the figures on the outside of the building. These include the "Grand Old Lady of Threadneedle Street" herself holding a model of the Bank in her hands.

Cross over the roadway and walk along Prince's Street that runs alongside the Bank of England's western wall until you reach Lothbury. Here again cross the roadway and, look back towards the Bank. On the opposite corner can be seen high over the wall of the Bank the gilt statue of **Ariel** (3). The work of Charles Wheeler, it was erected in 1921.

Walk along the pavement on the opposite side to the Bank, noting on the north face of the Bank's wall the statue of **Sir John Soane**, (4) 1753-1837, by Sir William Reid Dick, 1879-1961. It was placed there at the time when Sir Herbert Baker was rebuilding the Bank, and pulling down much of the work that Soane had been responsible for erecting in the 18th century.

The Parish church of **St. Margaret Lothbury** (5) was rebuilt after the Great Fire of London in 1666, but the records show that there was a church here in the 12th century. Little is known for certain about St. Margaret of Antioch to whom the church is dedicated, most of the stories about her are fictitious. They include the story of a pagan priest who had a daughter named Margaret, and because she refused the advances of the local Roman Prefect was denounced as being a christian. After which her ordeals take on an almost fairy story character, telling how she was swallowed by the Devil, who took the form of a dragon, and how, eventually, she was beheaded during the time of the reign of Diocletian and his persecution of the christians at that time. Her symbol is a dragon, and she can be seen overcoming one in the picture,(a copy of one by Raphael, 1483-1520,) that hangs in the entrance lobby of the church. This picture denotes her refusal to sacrifice to the heathen gods at the bidding of her Roman persecutors. The exact origin of the name Lothbury is lost in obscurity, but there are several suggestions as to how and why it received its title. One of the most obvious ones is that it is a direct derivation from the Norman landlord with the "bury" being taken from the Saxon word for a "large house" i.e. "bury". Another school of thought points out that near to the church the Worshipful Company of Founderers of the City of London were to be found, and there is still Founders Court a few yards from the church, and while carrying out their business made a "loathsome" smell. The fact that there was a church here in the 12th century is confirmed by the list of Rectors that hangs in the church today which shows that one Reginald the Priest was installed here in 1185. In 1440 the church was rebuilt, and at the same time the River Walbrook, which flows underneath the church, was partly covered over. Springs from Islington supply the river with water, and in the 17th century were used to supply water to the parish by the means of a conduit outside the building. This church was destroyed in the Great Fire of 1666, and was rebuilt between 1686 and 1690 by Sir Christopher Wren, 1632-1723. Today the church acts as the Parish Church to seven other churches of medieval London, under the Reorganisation Areas Measure of 1944. The new parish now covers the area from the Bank of England to London Wall, and from Old Broad Street to Bassinghall Street, and includes the former parishes of St. Mary Colechurch, St. Mildred Poultry, St. Martin Pomeroy, St. Olave Jewry, St. Bartholomew by the Exchange, St. Christopher le Stocks, and St. Stephen Coleman Street. Within the church there are numerous items of interest to the pilgrim in search of 'relics of former churches', and it has become an excellent deposi-

tory of furnishings from other Wren churches. When All Hallows the
Great in Upper Thames Street was demolished in 1897 the rood
screen, which had been presented to the church by James Jacobson
and his brother Theodore, German merchants, was removed and re-
erected here. It is one of only two; the other is in St. Peter upon
Cornhill church; to be erected in any of the City's churches since the
Reformation of the 16th century. The sounding board of the pulpit
came from the same church, although the pulpit itself is the one
designed by Wren for this church. Both are attributed to Grinling
Gibbons, 1648-1721, as is the font which is inscribed with appropri-
ate scriptural subjects, it was made originally for the church of St.
Olave Jewry, after that building had been converted in 1888 into a
Rectory House. On the credence table within the altar rails is a
gilded cross that was made from a piece of oak from Old St. Paul's
Cathedral. Under the portrait of Elizabeth I, 1533-1603, there is an
inscription which reads, "Elizabet, D.G. Angliae Franciae
Hiberniae et Verginiae Regina" that is "Elizabeth by the Grace of
God, Queen of England, France, Ireland and Virginia". The reredos
behind the altar has on either side of it two large paintings of Moses
and Aaron. These came from the Parish Church of St. Christopher
Le Stocks when the church was demolished in 1781. Note too the
bronze bust of Sir Peter le Maire who died in 1631, also from the
same church, and the tablet with bust of the great engraver and pub-
lisher Alderman Boydell, Lord Mayor of London in 1790 from St.
Olave's church. There is a small graveyard behind the church,
where there lies buried Sir Hugh Clopton, Lord Mayor of London
1491-1492, who died in 1496, and was responsible for the building of
the Clopton Bridge over the River Avon at Stratford in
Warwickshire. He also rebuilt the Parish Church of the Holy Trinity
at Stratford upon Avon, where William Shakespeare is buried in the
chancel. Lothbury soon gives way to Throgmorton Street and,
about half way along on the left hand side, is to be found
Throgmorton Avenue which passes underneath the **Worshipful
Company of Drapers Hall**. (6) The coat of arms of the Company
adorns the top of the gates that bar the entrance to this private way
once a year. The gate is usually closed on Good Friday in order to
maintain the right of way to the Drapers Company, and not to the
general public. By closing the gate for twenty four hours once each
year the right of way by the land owner is maintained. Note the coat

of arms that comprises three Imperial Crowns, similar to the crown that the Popes used to wear at their Coronation, but with sunbeams, these also form part of the coat of arms of the Queen Mary College of the University of London, who were given £100,000 towards the foundation of the college by the Company of Drapers. The Company motto "Unto God only be honour and glory" can also be seen on the arms. The Company, of trade guilds was among those who in Pre-Reformation days owed their allegiance to Our Lady, the Blessed Virgin Mary and who were incorporated in 1438 as the Guild or Fraternity of the Blessed Mary of Drapers of London. The entrance to the Hall of the Company is in Throgmorton Street and was rebuilt in the 19th century in the classical style.

Walk down Throgmorton Avenue, passing on the right hand side the buildings of the Drapers Company, with their garden at the end, and here turn to the right and walk into **Austin Friars** (7).

The monastery was founded in 1253 by Humphrey Bohun, Earl of Hereford and Essex, Constable of England, and god-father to Edward I, 1239-1307, "to honour God, and the Virgin for the health of the soul" of his father Henry III, 1207-1272, and his descendants. Originally the area covered by the Order was small but by the 14th century it was rebuilt in a finer and grander scale, by the grandson of the Founder, another Humphrey Bohun. The new church had a nave over one hundred and fifty feet long and eighty three feet wide, and so became the largest floor space in the city—at one time it rivalled Westminster Abbey with its large number of monuments and memorials. Within its walls were buried the famous, and the infamous. Edward, the eldest son of the Black Prince, and the Fair Maid of Kent were buried near the high altar of the church. After the Dissolution of the Monasteries in the 16th century the church was given to the Dutch Reform church, but they were allowed to use only the nave of the church. The rest of the buildings having been given over to Sir William Paulet, Lord Treasurer of England, and later the Marquess of Winchester who used various parts of the buildings as storehouses. He turned the choir into a coal store and sold the monuments and memorials for one hundred pounds. On the death of Edward VI, 1537-1553, and the succession to the throne of Mary, 1516-1558, and the return to the "Old Religion", the Dutch were ejected from the church and all protestant refugees were ordered to leave the country within twenty four days. On her death in 1558, and the succession to the throne of Elizabeth I, 1533-1603, they were allowed to return once more and have held their services there ever since, with a slight break in the Second World War, 1939-1945, after a land-mine had exploded nearby and destroyed the church. Princess Irene, the ten year old daughter of Queen Wilhelmener of the Netherlands laid the foundations of the present church building in July 1950.

From the church the street called Austin Friars twists and turns until the junction of Throgmorton Street and Old Broad Street is reached. Here cross the roadway and walk along the side of the **Stock Exchange** (8) on the right until a "blue-plaque" is found on the outside wall of the Exchange. The plaque was unveiled by Sir Ronald Gardner-Thorpe in October 1981, while he was the Lord Mayor of London. It commemorates the site of the birthplace of Cardinal Henry Newman in 1801, who was a key figure in John Keble's Oxford Movement that was to restore to the Church of England much what it had lost at the time of the Reformation in the 16th century. Ordained within the Church of England he became the Vicar, parish priest, of St. Mary's church in Oxford, and from here published the "Tracts for the Times" in which he, and like minded colleagues set out their beliefs. They secured a wide influence from these publications. The group were given the name of Tracterians but were later termed the Oxford Movement. The Movement's prime aim to restore to the Church of England its "High Church principles", and its chief object was the defence of the Church of England as a Divine institution of the doctrine of the Apostolic Succession and of the Book of Common Prayer as a rule of faith. Soon within the group there arose a set of people who tended towards submission to the Holy Roman Church; one of the group was John Henry Newman. He entered the Church in 1845, served at the Oratory in both London and Birmingham, and was elected Cardinal by Pope Leo XIII (1878-1903) in 1879. Cardinal Newman died in 1890, and is buried at Rednal, near Birmingham in the Oratorians graveyard, and in the same grave at Ambrose St. John.

On the opposite side of Threadneedle Street from the Stock Exchange are the **Royal Exchange Buildings** (9), a pedestrian side street which links Threadneedle Street with Cornhill at the far end. Here there is a "blue-plaque" noting the site of the Parish Church of St. Benet Fink. First mentioned in the early 13th century, the suffix "Fink" was according to John Stow in his "Survey of the Citie of London . . ." the result of Robert Finke's rebuilding of the church in the Middle Ages. It was burned down in the Great Fire of London in 1666, and rebuilt by Sir Christopher Wren between 1673 and 1676. It was here on 9th April 1801 that John Henry Newman was baptised into the Anglican church. Before leaving the area find in the ground the parish boundary marks of this parish and its neighbours. In the midst of the paved area, the site of the church, there now can be found the statue of George Peabody, 1795-1869, the American philanthropist, who founded the Peabody Estates with the intention of providing housing for people near to their place of work. The statue, the work of W.W. Storey, 1819-1895, was erected in the year of Peabody's death, 1869.

Cross over the roadway and walk along Threadneedle Street to the "blue-plaque" marking the site of **St. Anthony's Hospital**, (10) opposite Finch Lane. Formerly a synagogue the land was given to the brothers of the Hospital of St. Antoine de Viennois in 1254 by Henry III, 1207-1272, as their London home. From here they collected alms for the French Hospital that was established to treat those suffering from ergotism, commonly known as St. Anthony's Fire, and caused by the eating of poisonous grains of rye. They also offered hospitality to passers-by. In this they were assisted by the Corporation of the City of London, who gave them the right to acquire any pig, found wandering in the city, that had been deemed unfit to be killed for eating. This gave rise to the saying that "such a one will follow such a one and whine as if it were an Anthony pig" The last "Anthony pigs" were recorded in 1545. In 1414, under the Alien Priories Act, the monastic institution was dissolved, and a royal free chapel established in its place. Then, in 1440, with funds appropriated from the nearby parish of St. Benet Fink, a grammar school for boys was founded, which was to become one of the two main City schools. In 1442 Henry VI, 1421-1461, endowed the school with five scholarships to Eton and Oxford. In 1475 Edward IV, 1442-1483, gave the hospital to the Dean and Canons of St. George's Chapel in Windsor Castle, and although it was not dissolved by Henry VIII, 1491-1547, or, Edward VI, 1537-1553, one Prebendary Edmund Johnson of Windsor dissolved the choir, sold the plate, and turned out the almsmen in 1540. As a result the school declined and was finally, in 1550, let to the French Protestant Church who made it their home until 1840 when they moved to Soho Square in the West End. Among the many thousands of boys educated at the school were Saint Thomas More, 1478-1535, John Whitgift, 1530-1604, who was appointed Archbishop of Canterbury in 1583, and who opposed Puritanism, despite his Calvinistic background. An earlier pupil of the school, in the 15th century, had been John Colet, 1466-1519, a brilliant and austere reformer, within the Church prior to the Reformation. A close friend of Erasmus, 1466-1536, the Dutch humanist, and editor of the Greek New Testament, and of Saint Thomas More, he was Dean of St. Paul's from 1504 to 1519. He founded St. Paul's School in 1512. The buildings were pulled down in 1840 to make way for the road widening at that time.

A short distance from the site of the hospital, on the other side of the roadway, stands the Hall of the **Worshipful Company of Merchant Taylors of the City of London**. (11). Founded in 1326 the Guild of Merchant Taylors of the Fraternity of St. John the Baptist, as a result of the armourers and tailors petitioning Edward III, 1312-1377, to govern their own "mistery". The king granted their request by issuing a "letters patent" allowing the Company to make male garments, and, also naming them as makers of linen for the lining and quilting of armour. Their coat of arms over the great doorway to their hall shows a pavilion with imperial purple garnished, and either side two mantles also imperial purple lined with ermine, with supporters on either side of camels, while the crest shows the Holy Lamb within a sun. The Company's motto "Concordia parvae res crescunt", being translated as, "With harmony small things become great", is to be found under the coat of arms. Merchant Taylors are one of the Great Twelve companies of the City of London. The Hall of the company has stood on this site since 1331, although badly damaged in the Great Fire of London and in the Blitz of 1940, the restored hall retains much of the medieval building. Two other portions of the medieval building remain—the 14th century crypt to the chapel, and the walls of the kitchen which date from the 15th century. Among the treasures of the Company are two early 16th century funeral palls; elaborately embroidered clothes that were laid over the coffin of a departed member of the Company; together with a portrait of Robert Dowe who in the 17th century left money to purchase a handbell to be rung outside the condemned cell of Newgate Prison on the eve of executions. The practice has long since ceased but the bell still exists in the Parish Church of Saint Sepulchre without Newgate. Among the numerous charitable activities in which the Company is engaged is the maintenance of almshouses and flats for the elderly and infirm. It also supports schools including its own Merchant Taylors School that it founded in 1561 in Charterhouse Square, and moved to Northwood in 1933.

At the junction of Threadneedle Street with Bishopsgate, and on the corner of these two roadways stood the **Parish Church of St. Martin Outwich**, today the site is marked by a "blue-plaque", (12)—first mentioned in the early 13th century, when it was endowed by Martin de Ottewich and his family. It survived the Great Fire of London, but suffered in a fire of 1765. Pulled down in 1796, it was rebuilt by Samuel Pepys Cockerill, c1754-1827, who through the maternal side of his family was related to Samuel Pepys, 1633-1703, the 17th century diarist. He designed a small church with an oval interior. In 1874 it was demolished to make way for a banking hall. The parish was joined with that of St. Helen's Bishopsgate and many of the monuments were transferred to that church where they can still be seen today. The bones from the vaults of the church were re-interred in Ilford Cemetery, and include those of a certain Mrs Abigail Vaughan. When she died she left the parish an annuity of four shillings with which to buy faggots to be used for the burning of heretics. Turn right and walk along Bishopsgate to the junction of Cornhill, Leadenhall Street with Gracechurch Street (13). Here stood, until the 17th century, **"The Standard upon Cornhill"** that was used to measure distances to and from the City of London until its removal.

In Cornhill can be found the Parish Church of **St. Peter-upon-Cornhill** (14). Here, according to tradition a church was founded in 179 AD by King Lucius as a place of worship for the then archbishop. It is more likely that in a villa on the site, close to the Roman Basilica and Forum of Londinium, there was a chapel dedicated to the Christian Faith, and probably lived in by a Roman citizen who had been converted to Christianity in Rome before he left for duty in London. There is a brass inscription in the Vestry today that still tells the story of King Lucious and his foundation of the church in 179 AD. The plaque also tells how the church became the seat, cathedra, of Bishop Restitutus of London, how he made it his base, and how he attended the Council of Arles in 314 A.D. to discuss the

Donatist schism in the church. Donatists were a schismatic sect in the African Church who had refused to accept Caecilian as Bishop of Carthage on the grounds that he had been consecrated bishop by a traditor. Traditors in Africa were among those who had surrended the Holy Scriptures at the time of the Diocletian persecutions in 303 A.D. In 1417 the Lord Mayor and the Corporation of the City of London proclaimed St. Peter's church to be the oldest church in the City. This gave the parish a number of privileges including one that allowed their Rector precedence "on the Monday in the week of Pentecost" when the Lord Mayor and the Aldermen made a solemn procession from the church to the cathedral. Whether this was brought about because of the 15th century declaration of the church's age, or whether it was the result of being dedicated to the "Chief of the Apostles" is not known for certain. At the time of Henry IV, 1367-1414, a Guild of St. Peter was set up here, with the Worshipful Company of Fishmongers making up the majority of the members. The 15th century was an important time in the history of the parish. During that era Richard "Dick" Whittington, 1358-1423, was a parishioner here and attended the church regularly. In 1447 its Rector sent a petition to the King, Henry VI, 1421-1461, asking that the parish grammar school be allowed to stay in the parish's keeping. The school was recognised as being one of the best schools in London at that time. The medieval church had seven altars, and two towers, one of which was heavily battlemented. This church was destroyed in the Great Fire of London, and was rebuilt between 1677 and 1681 to the designs of Sir Christopher Wren. The church is smaller today than in Medieval times, due to the widening of Gracechurch Street. Today's church consists of a chancel with two side chapels, and a nave with side aisles and one brick built tower that is surmounted by a copper spire with the Keys of St. Peter as a weather vane on top of it.

Before entering the church by way of the porch in Cornhill look up at the building to the right of the entrance. Here can be found the "Unholy Trinity"—three devils! Placed there by the architect of the buildings that are either side of the entrance early in this century who lost a dispute with the Rector and Churchwardens, they record his personal feelings towards the people of the church. Inside the church there is much of interest. There are four steps up into the vestibule under the organ gallery, and here on the right hand side in the Vestry there can be seen the brass plaque already referred to earlier, the original keyboard of the Bernard Schmitt (Father Smith) organ on which Mendelssohn played in September 1840, together with his autograph and a manuscript of a few notes of music. Here too can be seen a long table, now utilised for a number of purposes, but originally a "withdrawing table", designed to be used for the celebration of the Eucharist. In order to make the point that the Holy Sacrifice of the Mass was no longer being offered by the Church of England at that time, it was made to be removed from the body of the church after its use. Hence a "withdrawing table". Return to the church once more, and turn right. Slightly above head height can be seen the Charity Bread Shelves, which are the relics of an earlier age when bread was given out to the poor of the parish after the main morning service on Sundays. Two other churches in the city St. Clement's Eastcheap, and St. Martin within Ludgate, also have Bread Shelves. Other furnishings consist of a Rood Screen, the second of only two Post-Reformation screens in the City, the other being at St. Margaret Lothbury. The pulpit and sounding boards by Grinling Gibbons 1648-1720, while most of the panelling is original too from the time of Wren's rebuilding. The 17th century wood can easily be identified by its colour. Wren ordered that all new wood should be first taken to the Meat Market at Smithfield, where in the slaughter houses and abbatoirs, the wood was to be allowed to soak in the blood from the animals. This has acted as a very fine preservative—none of the woodwork so treated has suffered from either dry-rot or the dreaded death watch beetle. On the south wall there is a pathetic monument with seven cherubs' heads, commemorating a family of seven children all of whom were burnt to death in 1782, while their parents were at a ball in St. James's Palace. George Borrow, was married here in 1840 and in 1843 wrote "The Bible in Spain", that tells of his adventures there while distributing bibles and religious tracts from 1835 to 1840. Each year shortly before Christmas the St. Peter's Players re-enact one of the cycles of Medieval Mystery Plays on a stage, in true medieval style, in front of the rood screen. They are well worth a visit. Before leaving the church say a prayer for the Recusants, i.e. those members of the parish who refused to conform with the Church of England in the 16th and 17th centuries preferring to remain loyal to the Catholic Church of Pre-Reformation times. In various returns made to the Privy Council in the 16th century there are reports of recusants in the parish. In 1577 there was only one Catholic reported and he was said to be "banquerupte and of no value". In 1584 in the house of one Thomas Forman, there lived a husband and wife, two men and two women servants, and four young children. Again no action seems to have been taken against them. In the house of Thomas Fox are to be found recorded a husband and wife, a boy and woman servants and three young children. They are "poor folk and no record shall be kept of them".

A short distance from St. Peter's church is to be found the Parish Church of St. Michael's Cornhill.

One of the earliest foundations in the City the **Parish of St. Michael's Cornhill** (15) was in Saxon times given to the Abbey of Evesham in Worcestershire who maintained connections with the parish up to the time of the Reformation when the patronage was taken over by the Worshipful Company of Drapers. It would seem quite appropriate that the Company should be so closely associated with one of the two churches that dominate Cornhill. Here in the Middle Ages was one of their main trading centres, the market on Cornhill, together with Birchin Lane that runs out of the street. They also are remembered by John Lydgate, c.1370-c.1451, a monk of Bury St. Edmunds who was "a most voluminous writer of verse", wrote "London Lickpenny" that gives a good contemporary view of London and Westminster in the 15th century. Of Cornhill and its occupants he writes:-

"Then into Corn-Hyl anon I yode,
Where was mutch stolen gere amonge.
I saw where honge myne owne hoode
That I had lost amonge the thronge.
To by my own hoode I thought it wrong.
I knew it well as I did my crede,
But for lack of money I could not spede".

The medieval church had chapels dedicated to St. Mary, St. Margaret, St. Anne, St. Christopher and St. Catherine, and it was during the Middle Ages that many of the parishioners left money for the foundation of chantries for the parish priests to pray for their souls, those of their families, and for the relief of the poor of the parish. Parochial records show that in 1340 one Roger Harold bequeathed to the church money to maintain torches inside the church. Presumably these were the only means of lighting the major part of the church—the altar only being lit by candlelight, the rest of the church in darkness except for the torches provided under this gift. A brewer, Roger Stockton in 1427 left his entire brewery to the church with a proviso that a candle be lit, and for it to burn continuously before the high cross which presumably was to be found on the Rood screen in the Pre-Reformation church, and for a "year's mind" to be kept for his wife and family. His premises were to be found further down Cornhill towards the Royal Exchange, opposite the Tun, which was the local lock-up, and next to which was "a fair well of spring water". A disused pump marks the spot today. In the Fifteenth century William Rus, Alderman and Goldsmith of the City, left money for the 'usual' charitable purposes, the poor, provision of lamps, commemoration of the departed, and also for the providing of "Singing-Bread". Translated from the French, "pain à chanter", it is the old name for large altar bread used in celebration of the Mass, because during the making of the bread chanting and singing, was carried out. One of the now defunct Companies of the City of London is that of the Waterbearers whose task was to fill their containers, which held three gallons of water, from the conduit on Cornhill and transport it to the homes of people living in the City who were not then linked to the water carrying pipes. The men could be distinguished by the towels that they wore, one in the front and one over their backs to keep themselves dry. In 1570 Robert Donkin, a merchant taylor, gave the Company's hall to the parish. In the same century John Lute, a clothworker, left instructions in his will of 1587 that he wished to be buried in the cloisters on the south side of the church. His bequest also included the preaching of thirty sermons to be carried out within two years of his death. In addition to other charities he left a sum of money to provide for a learned man to preach a sermon in the church on St. Luke's Day, and also for the distribution of clothing among the poorest of parishioners. Although the tower and spire survived the Great Fire of London in 1666, by 1715 it had become unsafe and had to be rebuilt. The architect, possibly William Dickenson, an architect in Sir Christopher Wren's office, chose to build in the Gothic style of architecture. It is said to be modelled on either the chapel tower of Magdalen College, Oxford, or on King's College Cambridge, and houses one of the finest peals of bells in the City today. There are twelve bells in the tower all of which were removed in 1960, when the three largest bells were recast and the rest sand-blasted and quarter-turned. They were then returned to the tower and re-hung on a cast iron frame. During their weekly practice peal the bells are rung by the Ancient Society of College Youths who were founded in 1637, and are the oldest surviving society of bell-ringers. there is an interesting inscription on the No. Ten bell which reads:-

"To prayers we so call
St. Michael's people all;
We honour to the king,
And joy to brides do ring,
Triumphs we loudly tell,
And ring the dead man's knell.
R. Phelps Decit 1728".

All the original bells were cast by the Phelps Foundry in Whitechapel.

Under the direction of Sir George Gilbert Scott, 1811-1878, the whole of the interior of the church was redesigned between 1858 and 1860, when he chose a curious application of the classical style to fit into a medieval arrangement. Among the items of particular interest inside the building are the font on which the inscription reads "Donum Jacobi Paul Armri 1672. Renov. 1860", and behind it the finely carved pelican in the act of feeding its young. The latter is attributed to Grinling Gibbons, 1648-1720 the well-known wood-carver and stone sculptor who worked for Sir Christopher Wren in St. Paul's Cathedral and elsewhere. Most of the other wood carving in the church dates from the 19th century and is the work of William Gibbs Rogers. His most outstanding work can be seen in the pew ends. Each of the ends are different and show representations of flowers and plants that can be found in the Holy Bible, with the churchwardens' seats showing the Phoenix rising out of the ashes, symbolising the Resurrection of Christ and the rebuilding of the city and church after the Great Fire. For his work on the pulpit and lectern, both of which were displayed at the Great Exhibition in Hyde Park in 1851, Rogers was awarded a prize. Part of the 19th century restoration by Scott included the paintings by Robert Streeter, or Streater, 1624-1680, who was appointed Sergeant-Painter to Charles II, 1630-1685, in 1663, and who is best known for his painting of the ceiling of the Sheldonian Theatre in Oxford.

They show Moses and Aaron. The church's musical tradition is well established. Its organ was designed and built by Renatus Harris, 1651-1724, in 1684. Among the many organists who have been Director of Music in this church was Richard D. Limpus, the founder in 1864 of the (now Royal) College of Organists, and who became its first Hon. Secretary. There are also a number of wall memorials to the Cowper family of William Cowper, 1731-1800, the poet.

Leave the church by way of the doorway in the north-west corner of the building. At the foot of the steps can be seen the War Memorial to those parishioners who died in the First World War, 1914-1918. The work of Richard Reginald Goulden 1877-1932. The whole memorial stands nearly eleven feet high, and consists of a small grey-bronze statue of St. Michael, with up lifted wings holding a sword in his hand, with four children crouching at his feet on one side and two animals on his right. Listed on the bronze inscription are the names of one hundred and seventy men, out of a total of over two thousand who enrolled here during the First World War, 1914-1918, who did not return. A copy, unveiled by Field Marshal Lord Plumer in 1927, can be seen at Neuve Chapelle. In the churchyard on the south side of the church were buried the father and grandfather of John Stow, 1525-1605, the historian, as was the father of Thomas Gray, 1716-1771, the poet, who was born nearby in Cornhill. A plaque marks the site of the building at No. 41 Cornhill. In the 16th century there was a preaching cross in the centre of the cloisters in the churchyard. John Stow's grandfather left instructions in his will that his ' body to be buryed in the litell Grene Churchyard of the Parysshe Church of Seynt Myghel in Cornhyll, between the Crosse and the Church wall . . .". Today the churchyard has become a garden of rest, and all traces of the burials have been removed.

Between the church and the churchyard can be found a "blue-plaque" marking the site of London's first coffee shop (16), at the sign of the **Pasqua Rosee**, the Easter Rose, where the Jamaica Wine House now stands.

Return to Cornhill and turn left, and walk down the hill until **Pope's Head Alley** (17) is reached. Passing on the way number forty one, the birthplace of Thomas Gray on the left hand side of the roadway, and on the opposite side just before the Royal Exchange building is reached the pump referred to earlier. Turn left along the Alley, and then look up at the keystone of the archway at the opposite end of the alley. It shows the crowned head of an unnamed Pope.

Here according to John Stow, 1525-1605, the London historian, there was a royal palace in the time of King John, 1167-1216, but there is no trace of it today. The alley takes its name from the Pope's Head Tavern that is first mentioned during the reign of Edward IV, 1442-1483, and which retained its title after the Reformation in the 16th century. It is shown on maps as late as the 18th century, when the whole area around it was developed. In a masque about Christmas, written by Ben Jonson, 1572-1637, there is a character who says, "I am Gregory Christmas, and although I come out of Pope's Head Alley I am as good a Protestant as any in my parish". In the 15th century an English goldsmith of London was challenged by a Spaniard that he was not "so cunning in workmanship of goldsmithry as Alicant strangers", and set about to prove it—he failed! Samuel Pepys, 1633-1703, the famous diarist, visited the tavern several times as he records in his diary. On one occasion after the Great Fire of 1666 when he visited the rebuilt tavern to admire the new paintings on the wall he comments, but briefly on them, paying more attention to the drink and food that he consumed. Earlier in the 17th century the alley was the gathering point for several booksellers, including John Speed, 1552-1629, the historian and cartographer. Before its demolition in the latter half of the 18th century the tavern was the scene of a brawl between two actors, in which in defending himself Thomas Quinn stabbed, and killed John Bowen. Quinn was acquitted but never returned to the tavern here.

At the end of Pope's Head Alley is Lombard Street and the Parish Church of **St. Mary Woolnoth** (18).

According to tradition there was a church here in Pre-Conquest times, and that the suffix "Woolnoth" is the name of the founder. The first mention of the church is from the end of the twelfth century. Woolnoth seems to be derived from the name "Wulnoth". It was only damaged in the Great Fire of 1666, and Wren was called in to repair rather than to rebuild, this task was left to Nicholas Hawksmoor, 1661-1736, who, in 1716 pulled the building down and set about designing a new one. He chose the Tuscan style of architecture, and built his church to resemble a Roman atrium in a plan that is almost square. In spite of the general rearrangement of the interior in 1876 by William Butterfield, 1814-1900, there are several items of interest worth noting during a visit, especially the fine reredos which takes the shape of a baldacchino. The organ was built in 1681 by Father Smith, 1628-1708, and was, originally, in the west gallery of the church. When the galleries were removed in the 19th century the organ was moved to its present position. On the north side of the altar is a marble pyramidal tablet commemorating the Rectorship of the Revd. John Newton, 1725-1807 "to the memory of the Revd. J. Newton, once an infidel and libertine, a servant of slaves in Africa, 28 years rector of this church". He wrote the epitaph himself. It was during a violent storm at sea when he faced certain death that he cried to God for mercy. He later left the sea, and after reading the works of Thomas à Kempis, c.1380-1471, "Imitation of Christ", a manual of spiritual devotion that is designed to help christians become perfect in Christ, he was converted. For nine years he prepared himself, under the influence of John Wesley, 1703-1791, the founder of the Methodist Church, and George Whitefield, 1714-1770, a Methodist evangelist, for ordination in the Church of England. Eventually he became the curate of Olney parish church in Buckinghamshire, where he served for fifteen years before moving to London in 1779. Rated as one of the greatest hymns of all time "Glorious things of thee are spoken"—it comes from the "Olney Hymns" 1779, and refers to Jerusalem as being the heavenly City. In another of his hymns "Amazing grace (how sweet the sound)" he is recording some of his own spiritual autobiography. He records how before his conversion he was "godless and dissolute", and that he was changed by the grace of God. He was originally buried in the church here, but was, in 1893, moved to the churchyard of Olney. Note the gallery 'ends' that have now been fixed to the walls of the church, since the restoration of the late 19th century. Earlier in this century the City & South London Railway Co., tried to buy the site for their extension plans for the nearby Bank underground station. They failed in their attempt to have the church demolished, but were allowed to buy land underneath the building in order to create two new entrances to the station. Look out for the cherubs over the doorways that lead down into the crypt and "Lift up your hearts", but mind your heads if you pass underneath them. The outside of the church blends into the "office-landscape" of the buildings close by, so that many a person has passed by without giving it a second glance. It would be a shame to by-pass the church particularly its interior with its Baroque touches. The

Parish is now combined with the Parish of St. Edmund King and
Martyr in Lombard Street.

Outside the west end of the church turn left and walk along King
William Street, and cross over the roadway to walk down **Abchurch
Lane** (19).

There are several theories as to how or why the lane was so named.
One relates to the fact that the church of St. Mary Abchurch (20)
stands on rising ground and so became known as Upchurch.
Another source, Harben's Dictionary of London, says that *Ab* was
all or part of a personal name, perhaps Abo, Abba, or Abbo, while
"A.N. Other's" opinion is that it is a personal name but that of an
early incumbent of the parish. The church is first mentioned in the
twelfth century. Here lived John Moore, author of the celebrated
worm-powder and who caused Alexander Pope, 1688-1744, to
write:-

> *"O learned friend of Abchurch Lane*
> *Who sett'st our entrails free!*
> *Vain is thy art, thy powder vain*
> *Since worms shall eat e'en thee"*

One of the many interesting features of the church is the dome with
its painting by William Snow. It is of an architectural design with
seated figures, depicting Christian virtues and graces. In the upper-
most portion of the dome can be seen angels singing in adoration,
with King David and his harp with St. Cecilia, at the organ, leading
the heavenly worship. God is represented by the sacred name Jeho-
vah, in Hebrew script, in the centre of the sky. There is also much
fine woodwork and particular note should be taken of the reredos
behind the altar, by Grinling Gibbons, 1648-1721. A letter, written
by Gibbons himself, was found in the parish chest in 1946, in which
he acknowledges receipt of the money for the carving of the reredos.
It would seem that he was paid one hundred pounds for "carving the
alter pecs". Note the paving of geometrical design on the south side
of the church's exterior which is on the site of the churchyard. As a
result of bombing in the Second World War, 1939-1945, a crypt was
discovered under the forecourt and is probably 14th century in origin. Another domed chamber was also found at the same time but
that is under the pews of the church. Leave the paved churchyard
and walk to the end of Abchurch Lane and turn right along Cannon
Street. First mentioned in a manuscript in St. Paul's cathedral

archives in 1180 as Candelwickstrete, it was the street in the City where the Wax-Chandlers, the makers of the bees-wax candles for the churches, etc., had set up their businesses, until they were evicted by the Corporation after complaints from their neighbours of the smells coming from their workshops. In 1667 Samuel Pepys, 1633-1703 in his Diary, first records the use of the name Cannon Street as being 1664.

Opposite **Cannon Street railway station** (21) is to be found inserted into the wall of a bank **London Stone** (22). This peculiar object is perhaps one of the City's most famous landmarks. No one knows its exact origin, but there have been many surmises over the years. It is most likely a Roman millennium stone, used to measure distances to and from the city in Roman times. It certainly played an important part in the city during the Middle Ages as William Shakespeare, 1564-1616, in his play Henry VI part two, has the 15th century rebel leader Jack Cade strike the Stone and declare "Mortimer is now Lord of this City". It is also known that important proclamations were made from the stone. The Druids claim that it is an ancient ceremonial altar the like of which can be found in other parts of the country. Until its demolition after severe damage during the Second World War, 1939-1945, the parish church of St. Swithun's London Stone stood here. The earliest mention of the church was in 1271, but it was rebuilt in 1420 by John Heende, who was a Draper and Mayor of London in 1391 and 1404. He was buried in the church "with a fair stone laid over him". This, and other chantry chapels and monuments, were destroyed in the Great Fire of London in 1666. After the fire it was rebuilt by Wren at a cost of £4,687. 4s. 6d. Among the monuments and tombs to perish in the bombing was one to Mrs Agnes Reid who died in 1685, and was, probably, the first person to be buried in the new church. Her epitaph read:-

> *"Virtue and beauty here doth lie,*
> *Her sex's sole epitome:*
> *They must have Musick, all the Arts*
> *Judgement to use; or want her parts.*
> *When such vanish, then what can save*
> *The most ingenious from the grave?"*

From the Stone it is a short walk to **Walbrook** (23), here turn right and walk along to the Parish Church of St. Stephen.

The River Walbrook that gives this street its name is first men-

tioned in 1104, and according to John Stow, 1525-1605, Survey of
the Cities of London and Westminster, ran from Moorfields,
through the City to Dowgate. Crossing Lothbury, passing underneath Grocers' Hall, and past the "Old Barge Tavern", where
barges were moored, and so down to the River Thames. A writer of a
"History of London" in 1803, claims to have seen the stream "still
trickling among the foundations of the new buildings of the Bank".
First mentioned in 1096 the **Parish Church of St. Stephen
Walbrook** (24), was, originally, sited on the western bank of the
River Walbrook, but was rebuilt between 1429 and 1439 on the
opposite bank. This second church was described by John Stow in
his Survey as being "the fair church of St. Stephen, lately built on
the east side of Walbrook, for the old church stood on the west side,
in place where now standeth the parsonage house, and therefore so
much nearer the brook, even on its bank". The donor of the 'new
site' was Robert Chicheley who was Lord Mayor in 1411 and whose
brother, Henry Chicheley, was the Rector, and later the Archbishop
of Canterbury, and Founder of All Souls College at Oxford. In 1453
in the crypt of this church was buried John Dunstable, master of
astronomy and music, and over his grave in the old chancel of the
church was placed a Latin inscription that read:-

*"Is enclosed in this tomb he who enclosed Heaven in his breast,
JOHN DUNSTABLE, the confederate of the stars. He knew,
Urania showing the way, how to unfold the secrets of the heav-
ens. This man was thy glory, thy light, thy chief, O Music; and
one who had scattered thy sweet arts through the world. In the
year MCCCCLIII, on the day before Christ's birthday, he passes
as a constellation to the stars. May the citizens of Heaven receive
him as a citizen, one of themselves."*

A manuscript collection of "Latitudes and Longitudes" written by
John Dunstable in 1438 can be seen in Lambeth Palace Library and
at the Bodleian Library, Oxford. Stow mentions several other monuments in the medieval church among which are to be found one to
"Thomas Southwell, first parson of this new church, who lieth in the
choir". The church was destroyed in the Great Fire of London but
the crypt was left undisturbed. Therefore John Dunstable and
Thomas Southwell's graves remain untouched by the years. There
were several chantries in the medieval church. In the records of the
parish we read that Lettice Lee, widow, gave to the Rector and

Church Wardens of St. Stephen Wallbrook church certain lands and houses to the annual value of £14.10s. to sing masses for the repose of her soul. William Adams gave £126.13s.4d. "to the intent to maintain a priest to sing for his soul as long as the said money would endure". The parish was originally given to the Monastery of St. John, Colchester, but later passed into the hands of the Lee family, who were great benefactors of the church. They in turn gave it to the Grocers' Company, who, with Magdalene College Cambridge are the patrons of the parish today. After the great Fire of 1666 Wren rebuilt the church, at a cost of £7,652.13s.8d, and it was considered to be one of his masterpieces. Within the oblong plan Wren has contrived an arrangement of columns or pillars, sixteen in all, eight of which support the dome, said to be a proto-type for St. Paul's cathedral, while the others form the nave and aisles. The church is the burial place of Sir John Vanburgh, 1664-1726, the architect of Blenheim Palace in Oxfordshire. High on the north wall of the church is to be found a small tablet that commemorates Dr. Nathanial Hodges, hero of the Great Plague of 1665, whose deeds of heroism are re-told in Harrison Ainsworth's, 1805-1882, Old St. Paul's, published in 1841. The architectural prowess of the building achieved much fame particularly in Italy as can be shown by the story of Antonio Canova, 1757-1822, who said that the three buildings he wanted to see most in London were St. Paul's cathedral, Somerset House, and St. Stephen's church by the Walbrook. While Lord Burlington, 1695-1753, a notable patron of the arts, was visiting Italy in the 18th century he discovered a church that he considered to be beautifully proportioned. He commissioned an artist to make drawings and to take measurements in order that he might have a church of similar proportions built in England. When they were completed he then discovered that the church, in Italy, was in fact a copy of St. Stephen's Walbrook in the City of London! In 1986 a new altar was placed in the church which was the work of Henry Moore, 1898-1986 and caused much discussion at the time of its arrival.

From St. Stephen's church it is a short walk to the **Mansion House** (25) the home of the Lord Mayor of London during his year in office. Until 1753 when Sir Crisp Gascoigne took up residence there, the Lord Mayors would use either their own houses or the halls of their livery Companies to entertain their guests. The site chosen for the house was that of the former Stocks Market where "fish and fowl" were sold, income from which helped towards the upkeep of Old London Bridge. The Mansion House, built between 1739-1753, is rated one of the best works by the architect George Dance, the Elder, 1695-1768, and is a building "spacious and dignified" with ample space for the various functions that take place here during the course of the year of the Lord Mayor's office. Chief among the ceremonial rooms is the Egyptian Hall, based on the conception of a hall by the Roman architect Vitruvius of the 1st century BC, and is the banqueting room of the House accommodating four hundred people. Other rooms include the saloon, old ballroom, drawing room and reception rooms all of which are "richly appointed", and may be visited by prior appointment. In addition to the residential and ceremonial apartments the Mansion House also has a court of justice, and cells in the basement of the building. The Lord Mayor is the magistrate of the court. The front of the house has a Corinthian columned portico, which can be used as a viewing plat-form from where the Lord Mayor can take the salute when troops march past, and also from where he takes the salute at the annual Lord Mayor's Show on the second Saturday in November. Above the portico, in the tympanum, is the sculpture by Sir Robert Taylor, 1714-1788, and is an allegory of the City, which is represented by a woman crowned by turrets and with her left foot on a figure of envy, and her left arm upon a shield carved with the coat of arms of the City of London. The river deity and an anchor on a shell-strewn strand symbolise the Thames and sea-going shipping, the life-blood of the City.

On the north-west corner of the Mansion House can be found the "blue-plaque" marking the site of the former **Parish Church of St. Mary Woolchurch Haw by the Walbrook** (26). First recorded in 1260, in 1442 it was found to be in a ruinous state and had to be completely rebuilt. In order not to cut out any light to the nearby stalls at the Stocks Market this second church was built slightly to the south of the original church and in consideration of this a grant was made to the rebuilding costs from the revenue of the market. The church was destroyed in the 17th century at the time of the Great Fire and not rebuilt. The parish was then joined to that of St. Mary Woolnoth. When the foundations for the Mansion House were being dug in 1739 the foundation stone of the church was found complete with its Latin inscription. In 1643 Parliament ordered the wanton destruction of the statue of Our Lady that used to stand in the Pre-Fire church as being idolatrous. Outside the church there once stood another statue that of Charles II, 1630-1685, riding on a horse, apparently made in the first place to represent John Sobieski, King of Poland, but the City, wishing to show their loyalty to the King at the time of the Restoration of the Monarchy in 1660, bought it. They then had the figure "converted" into that of the king, and a Turk at his feet changed into Oliver Cromwell! In his poem "A dialogue between two horses" written in 1674, Andrew Marvell, 1621-1678, engages Charles II's horse in a conversation with Charles I's, 1600-1649, horse. Woolchurch's horse takes the side of Oliver Cromwell:-

> *"I freely declare, I am for Old Noll:*
> *Though his government did a tyrants's resemble*
> *He made England great and his enemies tremble"*

To which Charles I's horse replies:-

> *"Ah Tudor. Ah Tudor, of Stuarts enough,*
> *None ever reigned like old Bess in the ruff"*

The latter was obviously a supporter of Elizabeth I, 1533-1603. Finally, the suffix of the church's title needs a little explanation. Stow writes that it was called after the "beam pleced in the church yeard, which was therefore called Wool Church Haw, of the Tronage, or weighing of Woll there used". Haw is a corruption of the Anglo-Saxon word haze, meaning an enclosed space. Haugh and hoo are also variants of the same original word.

From outside the Mansion House it is a short distance to the Bank Station where this pilgrimage around the City Centre "heart and pride" was started.

Martyrs' Way—Newgate to Tyburn, via Smithfield

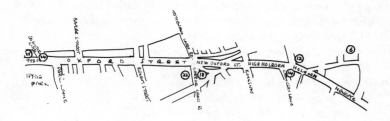

Martyrs Way—Newgate
to Tyburn, via Smithfield

We start from the "Old Bailey" which is only a few minutes walk from **St. Paul's underground station** (1).

Originally **Newgate** (2) was one of the gateways of the City Wall, that had been constructed by the Romans in circa 191 A.D., and was the west gate of the City—evidence of the gateway was discovered in the 19th century just north of the present roadway. It was completely rebuilt in the reign of Henry I, 1413-1422, and at that time assumed the title Newgate. During the reign of Henry III, 1217-1272, the City Fathers are recorded as having been directed, by the king, to pay Messrs Gerald Bat and Robert Hardel the sum of £98 3s. 10½d to construct a prison in Newgate. The gate was, once again, rebuilt during the reign of Henry V, 1413-1422, under the terms of the will of Richard "Dick" Whittington, c1358-1423, whose instructions included that the cells should be made more healthy than of late. Although the gate was destroyed in the Great Fire of 1666, it was soon rebuilt, and occupied by, 1671. To say that the prison achieved notoriety would be an understatement of the facts, the conditions there were appalling, as Father Garnet records when he was imprisoned in the most dreadful "cell" in the building—the Limbo—"it is an underground place, full of horrors, without light, and swarming with vermin and creeping things". The prison was to see during the 16th and 17th centuries many of the martyrs of the Church. Here were sent the ten Carthusian monks from Charterhouse who allowed themselves to be starved to death rather than submit to the oath of royal supremacy of Henry VIII, 1491-1547. During their stay in Newgate Margaret Roper, the daughter of Saint Thomas More, 1478-1535, came and visited the Carthusians here. Their names are part of the Roll of Honour of martyrs of the 16th century:-

6th June 1537	Blessed William Greenwood
8th June 1537	Blessed John Davy
9th June 1537	Blessed John Salt
10th June 1537	Blessed Walter Pierson
10th June 1537	Blessed Thomas Green
15th June 1537	Blessed Thomas Scryen
16th June 1537	Blessed Thomas Redyng
9th August 1537	Blessed Richard Bere
20th September 1537	Blessed Thomas Johnson

to which should be added the names of three Franciscan friars who were also put to death in Newgate in the 16th and 17th centuries:-

19th July 1537 Ven. Antony Brorby (Brookby)
July/August 1538 Ven. Thomas Cort (Covert)
Ven. Thomas Belchiam

In 1642 on the 8th April the Ven. John Goodman, a seminary priest and a convert to Catholicism died here having been found guilty of being a priest. Another secular priest who also died in prison at Newgate was Father George Gage. After his death on 28th July 1652 he was buried in the Parish Church of St. Giles in the Fields.

Before we leave this tragic spot it would seem appropriate that a moment of silent prayer should be allowed to remember all those who gave their lives, willingly, for the Faith that they had been taught to hold dearer than Life itself.

Newgate prison was demolished in 1902 to make way for the Central Criminal Courts that still occupy the site today.

On the opposite corner to the Courts stands the Parish Church of **St. Sepulchre without Newgate** (3).

Founded in Saxon times, the church was dedicated to St. Edmund, 841-869, king and martyr, King of the East Angles, who was executed by the "great hosts of Danes" who had taken up their quarters at Thetford in Norfolk. The king had refused to share his kingdom and was tied to a stake and "shot with arrows until his body was like a thistle covered with prickles". After the First Crusade in 1096 and with growing interest and participation in Church life, the title of St. Edmund and the Holy Sepulchre was adopted. The records show that the parish was given by Roger, Bishop of Salisbury in 1137 to the Prior and Canons of St. Bartholomew the Great in Smithfield under whose direction the parish remained until the Dissolution of the monasteries in the 16th century. In a recent move the parish has again been united with St. Bartholomew's Smithfield. In the reign of Richard II, 1377-1400, a Brotherhood or Fraternity, was established here in honour of the Immaculate Conception, although the Papal Bull on the Immaculate Conception was not issued until 1854, by Pope Pius IX, 1846-1878. A man named West, a joiner by trade, is recorded in Machyn's Diary as attacking, in 1554, the parish's Corpus Christi procession when the Host was being carried from St. Sepulchre's to St. Bartholomew's Smithfield. In the scuffle which took place, in which he tried to snatch the monstrance from the hands of the priest, he drew a dagger, but was quickly overcome by others in the procession and led away. Towards the end of the 16th century the Archdeacon of London, and chaplain to Bishop Bonner of London, one Harsfield, retired to a "house of a priest" in the parish and died there in 1579. Due to the nearness of Newgate prison it is not surprising that the records show that the church was often used by escaping prisoners from the prison. According to Canon Law any one who seeks refuge in a church may not, except by permission of the rector or the diocesan bishop, be forcibly removed from the building. In medieval times this sanctuary was often extended far beyond the confines of the church buildings e.g. Broad Sanctuary around the precincts of Westminster Abbey, which did not lose its rights of sanctuary until the 17th century—and then only after a great struggle by the Dean and Canons of Westminster.

In the Middle Ages the church had a number of altars one of which was dedicated to St. Stephen Harding c1050-1134, the third Abbot of Citeaux, who played a large part in the establishment of Cistercian Abbeys in this country. The saint was born in Dorset, went to Sherborne Abbey School, and as a young man travelled extensively in France. Eventually he entered into the Benedictine Order in Burgundy, which he left in 1098 to join the monks at Citeaux and where he became the third abbot having been one of the three founders of the Order. In 1112 the Order welcomed St.Bernard of Clairvaux into their company under whose late administration the Order grew in strength. All that is left of the chapel today is the piscina. At one time the parish supported a Fraternity of Our Lady and St. Stephen Harding.

At the east end of the church is to be found Giltspur Street, on whose corner built into the churchyard wall, can be seen one of the earliest public drinking fountains still in situ. Walk along the street, passing the parish **Watch House** (4) on the left hand side of the roadway. At the end of the street is **Smithfield** (5), the smooth field without the City Wall.

The Field was the setting for some of the most horrific executions of all times. Here Catholics and Protestants alike were brought by the judges and put to death by cruel means, in an area sandwiched at one end by the Hospital of St. Bartholomew's and the other by the Priory, later Parish Church of St. Bartholomew the Great. The open space was also used until 1855 for tournaments, fairs in particular, the weekly Horse Fair that was held on Fridays, and the great Bartholomew Fair that had taken place annually from 1123. Over the years this was the scene for over four hundred executions, and the most popular place to hang draw and quarter people, until Tyburn Tree took over the dubious honour in the reign of Henry IV, 1399-1413. Tyburn Tree was first used in the 12th century and was last used in 1783, during which time hundred of men and women were executed here. Catholic martyrs to be sent here include:-

1540 30th July Blessed Thomas Abel, secular priest, who was detained in the Tower of London, in the Beauchamp Tower where his inscription, the letter A on a bell can be seen, was hung drawn and quartered.
Blessed Edward Powell, secular priest and a former head-master of Eton College, was also executed the same way.
Blessed Richard Fetherston, priest and tutor to Princess Mary, hung drawn and quartered.

It was 50 years later in 1590 that the Venerable Nicholas Horner, a layman, tailor of London was hung for assisting priests in their duties.

Behind a small 13th century archway is the pathway which leads to the Parish Church of **St. Bartholomew the Great, Smithfield** (6). Founded in 1123 by Rahere, who while on a pilgrimage to the shrine of St. Peter in Rome, fell ill and in a dream saw a vision of St. Bartholomew, one of the twelve apostles. He vowed that should he recover from his illness, and return safely to London, he would build a church and hospital in the saint's honour—he did recover and

built a church and hospital. The earliest remaining part of the
church is the choir, the remainder of the church having been demolished at the time of the English Reformation and the Dissolution of
the Monasteries in the 16th century. Rahere, who died on 20th September 1143, was buried in the church on the north side of the sanctuary, where his canopied tomb can still be seen with the Latin
inscription "Hic iacet Raherus Primus Canonicus et Primus Prior
hujus Ecclesiae", that is, "Here lies Rahere, the first Canon and
First Prior of this church".

Although Rahere's tomb became a place of pilgrimage, particularly
for the citizens of London, and offerings and intercessions were
placed at his tomb he has never, as yet, been either beatified, or
canonised by the Church. His rebus, a play on a name in stone,
shows a tun, or barrel with a bolt, such as was shot out of a cross-
bow, passing through it can still be seen from the floor of the choir
today. After the Reformation the building was allowed to fall into
decay, with only the choir remaining and became the parish church
for Smithfield. It was, doubtless to this church that the Woolmen of
London would come for the annual Cloth Fairs in Smithfield,
accompanied by their Master and Wardens, with the Court of
Assistants to check the high standard that they required for wool
and its products. The north side of Smithfield is dominated by the
meat market (7) whose buildings were erected between 1851 and
1866, to the designs of the City Architect, Horace Jones, 1819-1897.
Walk through the Grand Avenue of the market, turn right, into
Charterhouse St. and shortly on the left hand side of the roadway,
will be seen **Charterhouse Square** (8).

Here under the trees of the square lie buried many of the victims of
the Black Death which had reached London in late September 1348
and spread throughout the City until November the same year. Records show that some 50,000 to 100,000 people are said to have died
during that time, and that the churchyards were soon full of dead
people. In desperation for burial space the City Fathers ordered that a large communal grave should be dug here in Charterhouse Square. The burial ground was given the title the "Pardon
Churchyard", and it was here that Sir Walter de Manny bought the
thirteen acres of land by the side of the burial ground and founded
the London house of the Carthusian Order. The Order was founded
at Charteux near Grenoble by St. Bruno who had himself retired

there to "avoid the corruption that was around him". The last Prior was, of course, Saint John Houghton, who was hung drawn and quartered, at Tyburn on 4th May 1535. Today the House is an almshouse for men—the Charterhouse having been bought in 1611 by Thomas Sutton who established a hospital for eight old men and a school for forty boys. The school moved to Godalming in 1872, but the old men remain in situ. In restoration work after the Second World War, 1939-1945, a curious fact came to light. For many years there had been great conjecture as to the purpose of a small slit of a window that can still be seen in the south wall of the church. It has now been discovered that by looking through this opening a direct view can be obtained on to the site of the original altar of the 14th century chapel, further investigations revealed the tomb of the founder of the Charterhouse, Sir Walter de Manny. His body was exhumed, and after careful examination, resealed in a coffin cased in lead and reburied with all due rites of the Church. Long may he rest undisturbed.

It is possible to visit Charterhouse, but only by arrangement with the Master.

Return towards Smithfield, and on the right hand side of the roadway will be found John Street, walk up the street, until the junction with St.John's Lane, leave the street and walk up the lane. Soon will be seen **St. John's Gatehouse** (9), this is one of the few buildings of the Order of the Knights Hospitallers left above ground.

Like the Knights Templars this Order was founded in the 12th century to protect the sacred places of the Holy Land. The gatehouse and the adjoining building is now part of the English Order of St. John, founders of the St. John Ambulance Brigade, the Order being revived in 1831 as the Protestant Most Venerable Order of the Hospital of St. John. Today the gatehouse and other buildings house the museum of the Order, together with the general assembly hall of the Order. The 16th century gatehouse was the last building to be erected prior to the Dissolution of the Monasteries in that century. It was in this area of Clerkenwell, whose title comes from the fact that the Worshipful Company of Parish Clerks of the City of London would come to the well here in medieval times and performed medieval mystery plays telling Bible stories. The Well can still be seen in **Farringdon Road** (10). Also in the same area executions took place in the 16th and 17th centuries. Just beyond the gatehouse, on 28th August 1588, Thomas Acton, alias Holford, was hung for being a priest, with the indictment reading "for being made a priest beyond the seas and remaining in the country contrary to the statute thereof". In the same year, 1588, Robert Sutton, layman and schoolmaster in London was also hung "for being reconciled to the old Faith". In the 17th century, Guy Fawkes who gained notoriety over the matter of the Gunpowder Plot was a frequent visitor to the area particularly visiting Thomas Sleep, a Catholic printer, as well as other recusants houses in the neighbourhood. For a short time in the latter part of James II's reign, 1685-1688, the convent of Clerkenwell was restored. On 11th November 1688 the rabble assembled and after committing "outrageous acts", and destroying as much of the property that they could before the foot guards were called in, left having killed a few in their counter-attacks. The riot was quelled, and the religious escaped to the Continent, and the remains of the buildings were raised to the ground and houses, etc. built over the site.

From the **Clerks' Well** (11) the main route of Farringdon Road, should be followed until, once again, Charterhouse Street is found. Turn right up the street towards Holborn Circus where the statue of Prince Albert, Prince Consort to Queen Victoria, can be seen. On the right hand side of the street just before the statue will be seen **Ely Place** (12).

Here is the last remains of the former London house of the Bishops of Ely—the chapel and which is now the Parish Church of St. Etheldreda's, and is the oldest Catholic church in use in London. The church is now the London house of the Fathers of the Institute of Charity, who bought the chapel in 1873 for £5,400, and who, after due restoration opened the church to the public in 1876. It is one of the finest relics of medieval London that can still be seen outside the two big churches of Westminster Abbey and Southwark (Anglican) Cathedral at London Bridge. Among the statues inside the church are one to St. Etheldreda, or St. Audrey, c630-679, who although married, twice, did not bear any children by either of her husbands and in circa 672 founded a double monastery on the Isle of Ely, where she died. St. John Houghton, Prior of Charterhouse in the 16th century, and who died a martyr's death at Tyburn, 4th May 1535, is also represented by a statue in the church. The crypt of the church was used in troubled times to house Catholics who were fleeing the law, and may be the original parish church for the area, with the upper chapel being used by the Bishops of Ely and private guests. One of the oldest possessions of the church is an ancient holy water stoup that is claimed to have belonged to a Saxon, or even earlier church on the site. For many years it lay buried, presumably to prevent its desecration at the time of the Reformation. By threatening to unfrock the Bishop of Ely if he did not part with them immediately, the house and chapel were 'acquired' by Elizabeth I, 1533-1603, for her favourite Sir Christopher Hatton, 1540-1591 and the land around was developed later for housing, etc. At the side of Ely Place was built Ely House, and here in 1605 came Dona Luisa de Carvajal, a Spanish lady of some note and wealth, who devoted much of her time to helping English Catholics in the early part of the 17th century. Twice she suffered imprisonment, and on one occasion was only rescued thanks to the unstinting efforts of the Spanish Ambassador, the Count de Gondomar. Her efforts to open a house for religious in London in the 17th century were thwarted by the King, James I, 1566-1625, and she was later confined to her house.

In Ely Court, off Ely Place can be seen the **Mitre Tavern** (13) which dates from the 16th century, said to have been built originally for the benefit of the Bishops' servants. The present building bears the date 1546, and contains in one corner of the bar, the stump of a cherry tree, around which Elizabeth I is supposed to have danced when on a visit to Ely House.

Return to the hustle and bustle of 20th century London, either by way of Hatton Garden or by Ely Place to Holborn Circus. Across the road-way can be seen the Guild Church of **St. Andrew Holborn** (14).

The exact site of the original church, founded c900 A.D. is not known but there is a record that Eolfric the Saxon dedicated a church to St. Andrew, the apostle here. This was once one of the busiest parish churches of 19th century London, but today serves the London Diocese as the centre for Education and Training. Although it was not destroyed at the time of the Great Fire of London in 1666, the fabric had fallen into disrepair and Christopher Wren, 1632-1723, was called in to rebuild the church—which he did, at the same time incorporating the medieval tower into his own one. In 1297 the records show that one Gladerinus, a priest, gave the "living" to the Dean and Chapter of St. Paul's on condition that the monastery of St. Saviour's in Bermondsey should have the care of the parish thereafter, and it remained under their care until the dissolution of the monastery in 1539. The size of the medieval church can perhaps be judged by the fact that there were at least four altars and it has been suggested that there might have been more than that number by the end of the 16th century. In the 15th century a grammar school was founded in the parish and there were other benefactions during the Middle Ages which include one by John Thane, who in 1348, left a number of shops and houses to help maintain the fabric of the building. The churchyard is the resting place of Blessed Swithun Wells a layman who was hung on 10th December 1591, at his own front door in High Holborn, close to Holborn Bar, at the end of Grays' Inn Road. He was found guilty of harbouring a priest in his house. The priest Blessed Edmund Gennings (alias Iremonger) was arrested while saying Mass and taken to Newgate still wearing his vestments and then hung at Gray's Inn Fields 10th December 1591. It was near the church either at the Bell or the Exchequer Inn that Blessed Thomas Holford (alias Acton, or Bude) was first detained. He was hung in Clerkenwell on 28th August 1588 as has already been noted. From Recusant Records one finds that even in the 18th century Catholics lived in the parish as may be seen from the will of Sylvester Jenks, priest, who died in 1714, and which includes "Iten the trunk of mine at Douai with what it contains I bequeath to the President of that College . . .my escritoire (writing table) to the Benedictine Dames of Brussels and the contents of Mr Richard Tobine . . . .".

Leave the church, cross the roadway and walk along Holborn and pause at the end of Furnival Street, previously called **Castle Street** (15). Here at number four lived Bishop Richard Challoner during the time of the Gordon Riots of 1780-1781. When the news reached the house that the rioters were on their way, his chaplain persuaded him to leave and to go to the house of Thomas Mawhood in Gloucester Street, near Queen's Square, where he died on 12th January 1781. He was buried in the family vault of his friend Brian Barrett in the village churchyard at Milton in Berkshire. The parish burial register there reads "Anno Domini 1781, 22nd January. Reverent-Richard Challoner, a Popish Priest and Titular Bishop of London . . . a very pious and good man . . . .". In 1946 his coffin was exhumed and laid to rest in the Chapel of St. Gregory and St. Augustine in Westminster Cathedral, London, where also can be found his mitre and faldstool.

Shortly on either side of the roadway, can be seen the columns on which the dragons of the City of London stand with the City coat of arms being supported by them. Here ends the City of London, at Holborn Bar a place like Temple Bar at the end of Fleet Street and the Strand, where travellers to the City would be stopped, searched if necessary and either allowed to pass on or were detained. Just outside the Bar people were executed at the junction with Grays Inn Road (Lane) and in 1590 the Venerable Alexander Black, a layman was hung for assisting priests in the neighbourhood. Here Blessed James Duckett stopped and received a pint of wine from his wife, which he shared with his betrayer, Peter Bullock, who was in the cart with him, also hung at Tyburn. He asked his wife to offer the wine to Peter Bullock and to forgive his betrayal of him. Blessed James Duckett had been found guilty of printing Catholic books. "So the betrayer and the betrayed passed in charity to their death" writes Canon Edwin Burton in his book relating to catholic streets of London.

Gray's Inn (16) was founded in the 14th century as an 'hospitium' for lawyers and since which date it has developed into one of the most important legal centres of London. Membership of the Inn has included the Blessed Hugh More who was hung in Lincoln's Inn Fields, on 28th August 1588, for being reconciled to the Faith, and Saint Henry Walpole who had studied law at the Inn, and was present at the quartering of Saint Edmund Campion at Tyburn, on 1st December 1581 when some of the saint's blood splashed his coat. This so stirred Saint Henry Walpole's mind that he left England, entered the Society of Jesus, and became a priest. On returning to England he was held captive first in York Castle and then in the Tower of London from where he was returned to York. On 7th April 1595 he was hung, drawn and quartered in York, and his head stuck on a stake on the top of Micklegate. It is ironic that a fellow student of law at the Inn in the 16th Century with these two martyrs was Thomas Cromwell, c1485-1540, who was to implement the Act of Parliament which brought about the Dissolution of the Monasteries in between 1532 and 1539. Cromwell was made Earl of Essex and beheaded in 1540 for 'heresy and treason'. During the 18th century

Bishop Milner lived in the Inn, and established a library for secular priests. Many of the books from this library are now in the library at Westminster Cathedral. Because of its quiet and retiring situation, in the 16th and 18th centuries Gray's Inn Fields became a meeting place for priests, which is probably why Saint Edmund Gennings and Saint Swithun Wells were both executed in the immediate area—as an example to any others who might be living nearby.

Further along High Holborn, on the same side of the roadway as Gray's Inn can be found **Red Lion Street** (17).

Here lived Bishop Richard Challoner in an area which in the 18th century became closely associated with Catholic lodging houses, Father William Elrington, formerly of St. Andrew's Holborn, but latterly of St. George the Martyr lived and died here in 1768. It was while Bishop Challoner lived here that the Gordon Rioters, having discovered that he had moved from Furnival Street, came and threatened to 'chair him and roast him alive'. We now follow High Holborn along until we reach St. Giles's High Street, and the Parish Church of **St. Giles in the Fields** (18) The origin of the parish lies in the founding of a Leper Hospital by Matilda, wife of Henry I (1068-1135) in the area bounded today by Charing Cross Road, Shaftesbury Avenue, and St. Giles's High Street. The chapel of the hospital served both the inmates and the people living nearby and at the time of the Dissolution of the Monasteries in the 16th century became the parish church in its own right. The list of Rectors of the parish date from this time (1547). The medieval church was replaced in the 17th century with one that was dedicated by Archbishop William Laud, 1573-1645, in 1630. In turn this was replaced by the present church, which was consecrated in 1734, designed by Henry Flitcroft, 1697-1769 in the fashionable Palladian style of the 18th century. The parish's part in the story of Catholic London is significant in so far as a number of martyrs who suffered at Tyburn were buried originally here in St. Giles's churchyard. Most of them were accused of being involved in the Popish Plot of Titus Oates, 1649-1705. Among them were five Jesuits-Fathers, Blessed Thomas Whitbread (alias Harcourt), Blessed William Harcourt (alias Waring, vere Barrow), Blessed John Fenwick (vere Caldwell), Blessed John Gavan and Blessed Antony Turner-all were hung drawn and quartered at Tyburn, 20th June 1679, and their mutilated remains interred here. Two years later, in 1681, Saint Oliver Plunket, Archbishop of Armagh, and Primate of Ireland, was dragged through the streets to Tyburn and executed. His remains were placed into a coffin by order of Charles II, 1630-1685, and buried here in St. Giles' churchyard, with an inscription engraved on copper which read "In this tomb resteth the body of the Right Reverend Oliver Punket, Archbishop of Armagh and Primate of Ireland, who in hatred of religion was accused of high treason by false witnesses, and for the same condemned and executed at Tyburn, the first of July 1681, in the reign of Charles II". Later his body was exhumed and taken to Lamspringe in Germany, the head is now at Drogheda and his body has once more returned to England and lies buried at Downside Abbey, Bath. It would appear from various records that are available regarding recusants in the 17th and 18th centuries that St. Giles's churchyard provided discreet burial space for a number of Catholics during those Dark Years of persecution. Registers show in their entries that "X" was buried with persons being described as "a gentleman" with sometimes the rider "reputed popish priest" being added, either at the time or in other instances later. On 29th July 1652, a secular priest, Father George Gage, was granted a funeral service at the church after which his body was carried away to a family vault. Wills that are filed in the Public Records Office tell of priests and their bequests. One such resident of the parish was John Leyburn, priest and bishop, who died in the 18th century and left bequests that included:-

£20 for masses to be said in the parish

£1000 to be paid to the college at Douai

£200 for weekly masses to be said at Douai and for an   anniversary sung mass

£20 to the Augustinian nuns in Paris and my sapphire cut ring left me by the Bishop of Chalcedon and presented to me by the Reverend nuns when I passed through Paris.

£20 to the Poor Clares of Dunkirk

His tomb in the churchyard has not been identified but like so many others "lies between the outward railings and the wall of the church on the north side". The Catholics of the parish were sufficient in number in the 19th century to found a school in 1829, in the High Street opposite the church.

Opposite the church was the **"White Hart" public house** (19) where the carts taking the martyrs and other to Tyburn would stop and the landlord would offer them a drink "to cheer them on their way". St. Giles's High Street formed, with the Oxford Road and Hog Lane (now Charing Cross Road), and Tottenham Court Road a very important, and impressive junction from early days. Here with the little village close by could be found, until the 18th century, a gallows, like others of its kind it was superseded by ones a 'little farther afield, and close to the outskirts of the City' in due time. It was common practice not only in London but elsewhere in the country, for gallows and scaffolds to be erected at the entrances in order to deter would be felons from entering the town or city. One of the medieval victims of the gallows here was Sir John Oldcastle a founder of the ill-fated rebellion of the 15th century which had begun in the previous century as a protest against the Churchs' oppression of its tenants. In its second phase in the 15th century the rebels turned their attention to more general social questions and became popular with the poor and needy classes. Sir John was found guilty of treason and heresy and condemned to death by being hung on the gallows here, over a slow burning fire.

Leading from St. Giles's High Street and the church is Denmark Street. Here in a small house in the 18th century were to be found some French priests who had left France "at the start of the trouble there". They were later to form part of the parish of St. Patrick's, Soho.

Through Charing Cross Road, and by way of **Manette Street** (20) enter into Greek Street, which as its name implies was once the place for a small colony of Greeks—whose chapel here was, presumably, Greek Orthodox—and so enter by the south side **Soho Square** (21). The square which takes its name from the more general title for the area, Soho, originally was called King Square after its founder. The very name Soho conjures up to some the origin of its name—when the area was used for hunting of wild animals the cry "Soho" was often heard—"So-ho" being the equivalent of the French "Tally-ho" as a huntsman's cry when chasing the fox. Dominating the square today, as it has done since it was opened in 1893, is the **Parish Church of St. Patrick's**. (22) The elegant church stands on the site of the house once owned and lived in by the Earls of Carlisle. In 1791 the house came up for sale and Father Arthur O'Leary, a Franciscan friar, arranged for its purchase and converted the former ballroom into a chapel—the first public Catholic chapel or church not attached to an Embassy to be used since the time of the Reformation. It was during the 18th and 19th centuries that the square became a haven for Catholics with the Neopolitan Ambassador setting up house here at number thirteen. At number seven in 1749 the Spanish Ambassador had a chapel built behind his house, "on the Oxford Road, side". Between 1749 and 1760 over 1500 baptisms and over 200 marriages are recorded as having taken place in this chapel, with the number of priests officiating here, as shown in the registers, numbering over thirty, with at least a dozen permanently attached to the chapel. This chapel and house was later to move to York Street and three years afterwards to Spanish Place, just north of Manchester Square, where a large Catholic church remains today. Bishop Richard Challoner was a regular visitor to the chapel and on one occasion in 1772 confirmed eighty Confirmation candidates there.

We join Oxford Street by leaving Soho Square by way of Soho Street. From here the way to Tyburn is straight ahead with few stops on the way.

Just past **Oxford Circus** (23), can be found Harewood Place which leads to Hanover Square, on the south side of which is the Parish Church of St. George, built in the 18th century at a time when London was spreading out towards Hyde Park. The church is of little interest today to pilgrims except for the fact that towards the end of the 18th century a survey of the parish revealed that there were one hundred and four known Catholic households, not persons, living there.

We continue to walk along Oxford Street towards Marble Arch and the site of the **Tyburn Gallows** (24).

On a triangular island at the junction of Edgware and Bayswater Roads with Oxford Street there is a commemorative plaque marking the site of "The Tree".

The first known execution here took place in the 12th century, and the last was in 1783. Between these two dates hundreds, if not thousands of people of all classes, religions both men and women, were put to death. In the latter days of its existence crowds of people would flock to watch the executions take place, a "Tyburn Ticket" being much sought, after exempting as it did the holder from any parish or ward offices. It was granted to successful prosecutors in criminal actions which terminated with capital punishment. The

Act of Parliament granting Tyburn Tickets was entered on the Statute Book in the reign of William III, 1689-1702, and was not repealed until 1818.

A list of the Catholic Tyburn Martyrs can be found as an appendix on page 130.

Close to the site, in the Bayswater Road stands the **Tyburn Convent** (25) which was founded here in 1903.

Driven from their home on Montmartre (the Mount of Martyrs) in Paris in the early 20th century by the anti-religious laws of France, the Benedictine Order of Nuns of the Adorers of the Sacred Heart found a home here, in a small terrace house.in the heart of London and close to one of the most important sites for Catholics. This settlement brought to fruition a prophecy made in the 16th century by Father Gregory Gunne who, while on trial for saying Mass, said " . . .the day will come that . . .you shall see a religious house built there (indicating the site of the gallows) for an offering". Today that house, rebuilt after destruction in the Second World War, 1939-1945, has erected a Martyrs' Shrine in the crypt chapel of the convent, where dozens of relics can be seen and revered from the Dark Years of Catholicism in England. There can be no better way to end this walk than to enter the upper chapel of the convent, where the Blessed Sacrament is permanently exposed, closely guarded in prayer by members of the Community, who are supplemented by members of the laity throughout the night sessions.

To which we can only add "Ora pro nobis".

Tyburn Convent
Tyburn Tree Altar in Relics Chapel

Lincoln's Inn Fields

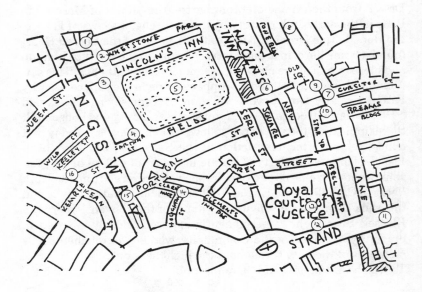

Lincoln's Inn Fields

Lying behind three of London's busiest streets, High Holborn, Kingsway, and the Strand can be found Lincoln's Inn Fields, an area full of history—both secular and ecclesiastical—to the inquisitive walker. We commence our walk from the Kingsway exit to Holborn underground station, and proceed to walk down the street.

Shortly on the left hand side will be seen the Church of St. Anselm and St. Cecilia, a building dating from 1909, with the south aisle being added when the new facade was built between 1951 and 1954. This church replaces the former chapel of the Sardinian Embassy which had served Catholics here from the 17th century. Incorporated into the church is an altar from the embassy chapel, as well as a large painting of the "Deposition from the Cross", which probably dates from the 18th century, and another altar from the Lady Chapel at Glastonbury in Somerset. How the latter altar-stone survived through all the years of persecution is unknown but it is there as a sure sign that the True Faith cannot be beaten into complete oblivion.

Walk along Twyford Place, at the side of the church to Gate Street, and turn left.

Here can be seen the Ship Inn (1), whose history can be traced back to at least 1549. As the inn could be approached from a number of directions it made a convenient spot for the holding of the Mass in the time of religious intolerances. Should the chance of detection arise of a hostile party coming one way, then the occupants could swiftly disperse another way. The cellars were large, and could, and did, hide many a priest from being discovered here. It was often frequented by Bishop Richard Challoner, 1691-1781, particularly

73

when he lived in nearby Red Lion Street, during the latter part of his life.

Almost opposite the inn can be found Whetstone Park (2) which in the 17th century was to acquire an unenviable reputation for vice and lewdness with, on one occasion the apprentices of London storming the houses in such a tumult that the local watchmen and constables were unable to quell the riot. "The Loyal and Impartial Mercury" of the 1st September 1682 records 'finding themselves unable to quell the tumult, procured a party of the King's Guards, who dispersed them'. But this was not so, of course, in the previous century when Bishop Challoner and the Charitable Society met here. Perhaps the Bishop should be best remembered as the person whose purpose it became to make the Douai translation of the Bible more readable to the layman. His work amounted "to almost a new translation" wrote Cardinal Newman 1801-1890. Cardinal Wiseman, 1802-1865, wrote 'it has been altered and modified until scarce any verse remains as it was originally printed". He used the King James's version of the Bible as a basis and in so doing the Bishop cleared up a number of obscurities that could be found in the original edition.

On the corner of Lincoln's Inn Fields and Remnant Street stands Newcastle House (3) built, originally, for William Herbert, the Earl of Powis at which time it was called Powis House. At that time the house became a meeting place for Catholic priests the Earl being the head of the Catholic aristocracy, and in view of the so-called Popish Plot, in which he was said to be implicated, was sent to the Tower of London for five years. On his release in 1684 he set about rebuilding the house that had suffered in a fire, but before it was completed James II, 1633-1701, had abdicated and gone into exile. Whereupon the Earl followed him to France and the house was bought by the Duke of Newcastle in 1705—and then became Newcastle House. Later the house was used by The Society for the Promotion of Christian Knowledge, the oldest of the Anglican Church's missionary and publishing organisations.

At the opposite corner of the Fields can be found Sardinia Street. (4) Here was the Embassy chapel whose present day successor is the church of St. Anselm and St. Cecilia in Kingsway. It was in the latter part of the 17th century that the Franciscan Order set up a chapel here, in a house designed by Inigo Jones, 1573-1652, himself a Catholic, and who in his late life was heavily fined for practising his religious beliefs. But even before the Friars set up house here Mass was regularly said by the Ven. William Harcourt, (alias Waring) a Jesuit priest living nearby. He was condemned and 'hung, drawn and quartered' at Tyburn, 20th June 1679. In a vain attempt to protect the Chapel James II sent troops there in 1684 prior to his leaving the country but they could not stop the mob from ransacking the chapel, taking away crucifixes, missals, and other objects of devotion and burning them in the centre of the Fields. The building was utterly destroyed and there is no reliable record of its history until the second decade of the 18th century at which time it became the Sardinian Embassy. Once again the site became a centre for Catholic worship in London, English and foreign Catholics alike enjoying the comfort of worshipping in the chapel. Under the Law which governed the exclusion of Catholic worship in England embassies were exempt being classified as 'foreign territory'. Bishop Richard Challoner was a frequent preacher in the chapel, but this was objected to by official sources on the grounds that it was not appropriate for the Bishop to preach in English to Sardinians! This did not, however, stop the good Bishop from celebrating the Mass, which was universally said in Latin at that time anyway from holding Confirmations. His preaching was then limited to being delivered at the nearby "Gate" public house that has already been mentioned. At "The Gate" the Bishop preached in the bar of the house, dressed in mufti with each of his congregation seated at the tables with a pint of beer in front of them-just in case the 'meeting' was interrupted by some official or other member of the Law. It was during this period of the 18th century that the chapel was frequented by Joseph Nollekins, 1737-1823, the sculptor, who was baptised in the chapel in 1737, and Doctor Thomas Arne, 1710-1778, the composer of "Rule Britannia", written for his masque "Alfred", although never described as a fully practising Catholic received the Last Rites on his death in March 1778. In addition to having written musical settings for Shakespeare's "Where the bee suck" and "Blow, blow, thou winter wind", he also composed two Mass Meetings specifically for the Sardinian Chapel. Once again the chapel was destroyed, this time during the Gordon Riots of 1780-1781 but was quickly rebuilt and became a centre well-known for the eloquence of its teaching and preaching. In the succeeding

century the chapel was often full to over-flowing with the congrega-
tion anxious to listen to the words of Doctor, later Cardinal,
Nicholas Wiseman, 1802-1865, and in particular his lectures on
"The Principal doctrines and practices of the Catholic Church"
which, possibly led Robert Browning, 1812-1889, to write the poem
"Bishop Blougram's apology". Some say that the poem was a mild
attack on the good doctor and of his changing from the Church of
England to the Church of Rome. Read it and decide for yourself.
The chapel was finally pulled down in 1909, when after the last Mass
was celebrated here on the 6th July that year and Benediction had
been given the entire congregation stood up and moved to the chancel and each, in turn, knelt down and kissed the floor before leaving
for the last time. Shortly afterwards the church in Kingsway was
opened, and the Faith continues to be taught in an area closely associated with Catholicism for over three hundred years at least.
Cross over the roadway and walk along the south side of the Fields
and walk to the centre where a wooden shelter (5) can be found, on
the floor of which will be seen a brass plaque commemorating the
execution there in 1683 of William Russell for his part in the Rye
House Plot. The Plot, was allegedly set up to assassinate Charles II,
1630-1685, and to replace him with William of Orange, 1650-1702, a
known and staunch supporter of the Protestant Churchmen. William finally came to England in 1688 at the time of the Glorious Rev-
olution when he accepted invitation from the Parliaments of both
England and Scotland to rule jointly with his wife Mary II, 1650-
1694. It was shortly after the future king and queen landed at
Brixham that the nearby Embassy Chapel was attacked, and the fittings burnt in the centre of the Fields. But the execution of William
Russell was not a case in isolation. The Fields, so near London and
yet outside it, was a popular place for executions in the 16th century. In 1586 Chideock Tichborne was executed here. He was
implicated in a plot to assassinate Elizabeth I, 1533-1603, for which
he apparently, had the blessing of the Pope, Sixtus V, 1521-1590,
(best remembered for his reorganisation of the Curia into the modern Papal administrative system.) One of the leaders of the Plot was
Anthony Babington, a young Derbyshire gentleman, who was
closely associated with the Society of Jesus, and who was to give his
name to the plot—i.e. The Babington Plot. The plan was not only to
assassinate Elizabeth I, but also Mary Queen of Scots, 1542-1587,

and so call for a general rising of Catholics throughout both of the Kingdoms. But Sir Francis Walsingham's intelligence service was second to none and the plot was soon discovered and the culprits, fourteen of them in all, brought to trial and committed to the Tower of London. Having all been found guilty they were taken to Lincolns Inn Fields and executed over a period of two days, 20th and 21st September 1586. On the eve of his execution Chideock Tichbourne wrote. "My prime of youth is but a frost of cares", and is a beautiful poem that is sometimes, quite wrongly attributed to Sir Walter Raleigh, c1552-1618, who himself resided in the Tower of London for a few years. The last line of each of the three verses of the poem reads "And now I live, and now my life is done". In another poem, "Arthur Babington, his Complaynt", the poet writes:-

"In the fields near Lincoln's Inn, a stage was sett up,
And a mightie high gallows was rayled on the same."

Isaac D'Israeli, 1766-1848, and the father of Benjamin Disraeli, 1804-1881, Prime Minister in 1868 and from 1874-1880, wrote in his "Curiosities of Literature", 1791-93 and 1823, that Father Ballard was executed first and was snatched alive from the gallows to be disembowelled, while Babington looked on with an undaunted countenance.

Two years later, in August 1588 on a new pair of gallows set up in Lincoln's Inn Fields Blessed Robert Morton, a seminary priest from Yorkshire, who had only been ordained the previous year in Rome, was hung for being a priest. At the same time Blessed Hugh More, a Layman from Grantham, and a member of Gray's Inn was also hung for being reconciled.

At the further end of the Fields can be found Lincoln's Inn (6). It was here that the Dominican Friars first settled when they arrived in London in 1221, "without the wall of the city by Oldbourne", on land owned by the Earl of Lincoln. Later this land was leased to the "men of law and their students". On the death of the Earl in 1313 the Professors of Law bought the land and so Lincoln's Inn was established. The "Inn" is private property, and the public have no right of access only privilege which means that if the gate is closed only those persons living or working there may enter. When the visitor does gain access they immediately find themselves in 'another world'. To wander through from the "Fields" side of the "Inn", past the 19th century gatehouse, the visitor is shown three periods of develop-

ment at once. On the left hand side is the Hall and Library dating
from 1843—look for the date and the initals PH on the end of the
hall—Philip Hardwick, 1822-1892, was the architect; while on the
right-hand side is the "New" square that was built in the 17th century. Looking, and walking, in a straight line, one finds the chapel,
designed by Inigo Jones, 1573-1652, who also first laid out Lincoln's
Inn Fields in 1618. In order to accommodate the 'men of law and
their students' in inclement weather the chapel was raised up over a
series of arches, the chapel itself being approached by two short
flights of steps over them. The chapel was built to replace the medieval building that had become too small and was in need of urgent
repair in 1619. The Preacher of the Inn was John Donne, the Dean of
St. Paul's Cathedral, who was born c 1572 and died in 1631, when he
was buried in Old St. Paul's he laid the foundation for the new
chapel in 1620. In 1623 the chapel was consecrated by the Bishop of
London, George Mounteine, or Mountaigne, with John Donne
preaching'a right and rare sermon' about dedications. Records
show that Price the Joyner was responsible for the interior fittings,
most of which survive today. Four of the side windows contain
stained glass made by the Van Linge brothers, Abraham and
Bernard, two Dutchmen who had been encouraged to work in this
country by Archbishop George Abbot, and Archbishop William
Laud, 1573-1645, and whose fine work can also be seen at several of
the University of Oxford chapels. In the immediate area of the
chapel the old hall of the Inn can be seen.
We leave the Inn by way of the gateway opposite the old hall, and
enter Chancery Lane. (7)
At the north end of Chancery Lane was the London house of the
Bishops of Lincoln in medieval times. Here (8) on 17th November
1200 died St. Hugh of Lincoln, c1135-1200, as he lay on a cross of
blessed ashes spread on the ground, and saying the "Nunc
Dimittis". There is no trace of the house today, which, according to
John Stow, 1525-1605, in his "Survay of the City of London", first
published in 1598, was built about 1147 by Robert de Curars, and
was on the site of the original London home of the Knights
Templars. Also in the lane lived Arden Waferer, a barrister of the
Inner Temple, who in 1570 was disbarred from practising his legal
activities "because of his Faith".
His house was often searched for catholic literature, as were the

chambers of a Lancashire youth named Norryce. Both houses were also "suspect of housing priests", and searched on a number of occasions for any priest hiding there—the tenants having received due warning they had made an escape before the searchers arrived. The gateway through which we left Lincoln's Inn (9) was built in the 16th century and is said to include among its bricklayers Ben Jonson, 1572-1637, who after leaving Westminster School was, for a short time, employed by his step-father as a bricklayer. The Chronicler of the story also records that he had a brick in one hand and a book in the other. Jonson, poet and dramatist, embraced the Catholic Faith "but did not persevere".

Walk down Chancery Lane until Chichester Rents is reached (10). Here was to be found the London house of the Bishops of Chichester. Of this palace Stow writes "The King (Henry III, 1207-1272) granted to Ralph, Bishop of Chichester, Chancellor, the place with garden that John Herlison forfeited in that street called New Street (Chancery Lane)" Chichester Rents, and Bishop's Court are modern day street names that are reminders of the former occupants of this part of Chancery Lane. Mathew Paris a 13th century monk of St. Alban's Abbey, Hertfordshire, in his "Chronica Majora", records that "Ralph de nova villa, or Neville, Bishop of Chichester and Chancellor of England, sometime builded a noble house even from the grounde, not far from the New Temple and House of Conuertes in which place hee deceased in the yeare 1244." Ralph Neville's successor at Chichester was St. Richard of Chichester, 1197-1253, who after being Chancellor to St. Edmund of Abingdon, 1170-1240, at Canterbury Cathedral was made Bishop of Chichester in 1244. St. Richard's successor at Chichester, John of Clymping appears to have spent most of his time at Chichester, 1235-1262, engaged with the remarkable growth of stories about the miraculous powers and saintly life of his immediate predecessor. It was left to his successor, Stephen of Berghsted to persuade the Pope, Urban IV, to canonise Richard, which he did in 1276. John of Clymping's only other claim to fame lies in the fact that he had erected across the Lane "two staples with one bar across the said lane, whereby men with carts and other carriages could not pass". Is this the first case of creating a pedestrian precinct?

Another of the Catholic martyrs who at some time lived in Chancery Lane was Blessed Thomas Sherwood who was a woollen draper by trade. He was arrested on his way to Douai, where he was to have studied to become a priest, and condemned to be hung, drawn and quartered at Tyburn, 7th February 1578. Others in the time of Elizabeth I, 1533-1603, who helped priests here included one George Gilbert, who with several of his Catholic friends arranged for lodgings to be available for the saying of daily Masses.

At the end of the Lane where it meets Fleet Street (11) turn right and walk along the street to the Royal Courts of Justice (12).

The Courts which deal with cases in the Divorce, Probate and Admiralty Division of Civil Law were built in the 19th century to the designs of George Edmund Street, 1824-1881, to replace these courts that had been held since the 13th century in the great Hall at the Royal Palace of Westminster. There are over one thousand rooms in the building, which consists of thirty-five million bricks with an outward face of stone, there are over two miles of corridors, and the building had cost £1.4 million pounds when it was opened by Queen Victoria, 1819-1901, on 4th December 1882. Standing high above the main—The Strand—entrance can be seen the figure of Christ, with His hand raised in blessing. On His right hand stands Solomon, King of Israel, the son of David and Bathsheba, who built Israel's first perfect Temple in Jerusalem, he holds a model of the building in his hands. In deference to Solomon's "Perfect Temple" Street designed these Courts to be imperfect with a column at the far end of the Great Hall with part of its decoration left undone to this day. On Christ's left hand stands the statue of King Alfred the Great, c848-901, whose enforcement of Law and Order was to lay the foundation for the Laws of England. His firmness in ruling led others in later times of trouble to say how they longed for the laws of King Alfred. Here overlooking the busy streets of London are three of the greatest lawgivers of all time. The fourth, Moses, complete with the two Tablets of the Law stands at the other end of the Great Hall overlooking Carey Street and Lincoln's Inn (13). Inside the Great Hall, which is 238 feet in length, 38 feet wide, and 80 feet high, stands the statue of Lord Chief Justice Russell, 1832-1900, who was the Attorney-General from 1886-1892, and became the first Catholic Lord Chief Justice of England since the time of Saint Thomas More in 1535. The moulding over the main archway to the Courts consists of over twenty four bishops and scholars through the ages.

Continue to walk past the Royal Courts of Justice, and along to the Aldwych and to Houghton Street, turn right into the street, and, pass on the left the London School of Economics and Political Science, until Clare Market is reached (14).

The market was established here in the 17th century on land owned by the Earl of Clare, John Holles, who obtained Parliamentary permission to develop the site for housing and the market. The Bill which was debated in Parliament in the 1650s caused a certain Mr Pedley to make some personal comments about the earl, viz "he (the earl) was one of those who had forsworn the building of churches—saying that he had built a house for flesh (referring to the butchers' shops in the market) but that he doubted he would hardly do as David did, build a house for the spirit". The market and the immediate area also developed into a 'rookery' a place where thieves, murderers, and vagabonds frequented, and where they formed themselves into a 'commune' for their own welfare. Later, the market was disbanded and the St. Clement's Workhouse erected on the site. Here also met the "Charitable Society", in the days of Bishop Richard Challoner, in a "miserable ruinous apartment in Clare Market". Portugal Street was the scene of the last public stocks in London, last used in 1820. The street, named after the Queen of Charles II, 1630-1685, Catharine of Braganza, leads to Kingsway. (15)

Turn right and walk up the street towards Holborn underground station. On the opposite side of the roadway can be seen Wild Street, (16) It was in Wild Street, named after Hunphrey Weld whose family built a house here in 1640, lived and died, the Venerable Edward Mico (alias Harvey) a Jesuit priest who was ordained in Rome and admitted into the Society of Jesus (SJ) in 1650. He was arrested in 1678 and charged with being involved in "The Plot"—Titus Oates "Popish Plot" of 1678—and found to be guilty. He was too ill to be moved and he died in Wild (Weld) House on 4th November 1678. When the street was demolished, prior to rebuilding c. 1800 many of the inhabitants were Catholics and had to find other safe places in which to live. It was also here, in the chapel of a group of Franciscan Friars that Father Arthur O'Leary served for many years, before moving to St. Patrick's Church in Soho Square. From here it is a short walk to Holborn underground station where the walk started.

Medieval Catholic London

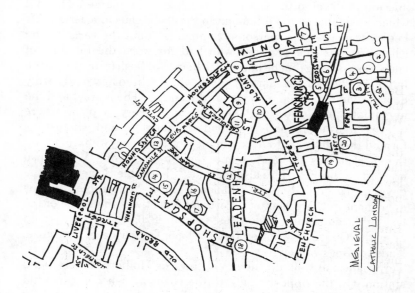

1 Tower Hill underground station
2 City Wall
3 Trinity House
4 Cooper's Row
5 Crosswall Street
6 Crutched Friars public house
7 Minories
8 Aldgate
9 Holy Trinity Priory
10 Aldgate Pump

11 St. Katharine Creechurch
12 St. Andrew Undershaft
13 "Papey"
14 Parish Clerks Company
15 St. Ethelburga
16 St. Helen's Bishopsgate
17 Crosby Hall, site of
18 Cornhill Standard
19 All Hallows Staining
20 St. Olave, Hart Street

Medieval Catholic London

Before leaving **Tower Hill** (1) underground station to commence the walk turn left at the entrance to the station and find the old **City Wall** (2). Near here was the Tower Postern gateway into the City of London in Roman times, and close by to the postern was to be found the Chapel of St. Mary and St. Nicholas. It was first mentioned in the reign of Henry III, 1208-1272, when it served as part of All Hallows by the Tower parish, and, in addition, acted as guardian to the postern where pedestrians using the gate could offer a prayer on their travels "beyond the City".

But return to the entrance to the station, pause, to look across the gardens of Trinity Square, and to remember countless souls who met their Maker after being executed on the scaffold erected here. Here also in the square can be seen **Trinity House** (3), the Brotherhood or Fraternity of the Most Glorious and Undivided Trinity and St. Clement, which was founded by Henry VIII, 1491-1547, in 1514. Its purpose was, and still is, the protection of the coastline of England and Wales by providing lighthouses, light ships and navigational buoys and beacons

Leave Trinity Square by way of **Coopers' Row** (4) where once the barrel makers set up their workshops. Just before the railway bridge which carries the trains in and out of nearby Fenchurch Street Station, in 1511, Sir John Milborne Draper, Lord Mayor of London in 1521, set up the Milborner Almshouses. They were demolished in 1862 and moved to Tottenham, the site then being developed for commercial purposes. Pass underneath the railway bridge, and turn right into **Crosswall Street** (5).

Known originally as John Street, after King John, 1167-1216, and following an Act of Parliament in 1760 "for the opening of streets to be made in the City of London", it was changed earlier in this century to Crosswall Street because it crosses over the City wall here. Shortly after entering Crosswall Street can be found the **Crutched Friars public house** (6).

In the immediate area of the house of today was to be found, in the Middle Ages, the London house of the Order of the Holy Cross, Founded in London in 1298, they were given land here in the early 14th century by Messrs Ralph Hosiar and William Sabernes. The Order was originally founded in Bologna by Gerard, the Prior of Sta. Maria di Morello, in 1169. The habit was at first grey but later changed to blue, on which they wore a red (leather) cross—hence they became known as the Crossed or Crutched Friars. At the time of the Reformation, and the Dissolution of the Monasteries, their land stretched to Seething Lane, on the site of which Sir Thomas Wyatt, the elder, built himself a most magnificent mansion, and where in the 17th century there arose the Navy Office, that was presided over by Samuel Pepys, 1633-1703. The refectory of the priory was turned into a glass conservatory and was the first to be erected in England.

A short distance away are the **Minories** (7).

The street which bears the name the Minories today is so called from the fact that the Order of St. Clare was founded here in 1293 by Blanche of Navarre, wife of Edmund, Earl of Lancaster and were known as the Poor Clares, or the Second Order of St. Francis, (of Assisi), 1181-1226. St. Francis himself had founded the Friars Minor 1210, who were authorised by Innocent III, 1161-1216, with his eleven companions to be roving preachers of Christ. They enjoyed many privileges during their time in London when shortly after they had been established Boniface VIII, who was Pope from 1294 to 1303, issued three Bulls in which he exempted the house from the jurisdiction of the Archbishop of Canterbury and the Bishop of London, and took them under his own care and protection. Later, in the reign of Henry IV, 1367-1413, the house was freed from the authority of the judges, mayor, sheriffs, bailiffs and coroners, except in the case of treason, the last being of course, their downfall at the time of the English Reformation and the Dissolution of the Monasteries. The strength of the house can be seen in the fact that in 1515 no less than 27 sisters and as many, if not more lay sisters were the fatal victims of a plague that went through the convent. At the Dissolution in 1539 the land passed into the hands of the Bishop of Bath and Wells, Bishop Knight, 1541-1547, and the buildings used for a variety purposes including an armoury and other secular uses. The church of the convent was used by the parishioners as their parish church with the title of Holy Trinity, Minories, this was demolished in 1740, and replaced by another building which has also now been pulled down.

At the end of the Minories stood one of the oldest of the City gates **Aldgate** (8), its name probably being a derivation of old-gate. Although there is a reference to AEstgate in the Anglo-Saxon Chronicle, part may have been written during the reign of King Alfred, c 848-901, and was compiled by the monks notably of Winchester, Canterbury and Peterborough, and which suggest that it might have been simply called the Eastgate from its geographical position on the eastern side of the City of London. It was not until the 14th century that the title in its present form appears in documents. Its place in the medieval history of London is significant in so far as from this gate ran the roadway from London to Colchester, another important Roman city (Camulodunum). In excavations undertaken after the Second World War, 1939-1945, a thick layer of burnt wood ash was found some eighteen feet under the present day level which was "concrete" proof of the firing of London in the 1st century.

Later during the Middle Ages, the gate was to 'see' Thomas the Bastard of Fauconberg, and a rebel force of some five thousand demand entry to the City—they were refused. Few of the rebels managed to penetrate the gate before the portcullis could be lowered, but those who did succeed were "quickly slain by the inhabitants". Shortly afterwards the Alderman of the Ward together with the Recorder of the City sallied forth and "with sharp shot, and fierce fight, put their enemies back so far as St. Botolph's church" at which time relates Stow, the Earl rivers, together with fresh forces from the Tower of London joining together to the discomfort of the rebels "put them to flight", and all were slain. In the 14th century Geoffrey Chaucer, 1340-1400, was leased the rooms over the gate when he was the Comptroller of Customs and Subsidy of wool, skin and tanned hides in the Port of London. The gate alongside the other seven were all demolished in the latter part of the 18th century—they got in the way of the traffic even in those days!

Just inside Aldgate was the **Priory of the Holy Trinity** (9). Henry I, 1068-1135, having succeeded his elder brother in 1100 he married Matilda of Scotland, who on the advice of St. Anselm, c1033-1109, who was Archbishop of Canterbury from 1093 to 1114, obtained a Papal Bull from Innocent II, 1130-1143, to found the priory here. The Bull refers to the absorption of four parishes within the precinct of the priory viz. St. Mary Magdalene, St. Michael, St. Catherine's and Holy Trinity, which existed here prior to the setting up of the priory. The priory became one of the most important monastic houses in London during the Middle Ages, and performed a number of civic duties which included the care of Aldgate. John Stow writes "this priory, in process of time, became a very fair and large church, rich in lands and ornaments, and passed all the priories in the city of London or shire of Middlesex; the prior whereof was an alderman of London, to wit, of Portsoken ward. These priors have sitten and ridden among the aldermen of the city of London, in livery like unto them, saving that his habit was in the shape of a spiritual person, as I have seen in my childhood". Stow also lists some of the important people that were buried in the cemetery here, which includes Henry Fitzalwine, mayor of London in 1213, Baldwin, the son of Henry I and Queen Matilda, as well as Geffrey Mandeville in 1215. In the course of over four hundred years of existence the priory developed its land ownership, and had its rights and claims acknowledged by Popes and Kings alike. On one occasion in the 13th century when the then Archbishop of Canterbury, Boniface of Savoy, 1245-1270, issued a summons against the Prior, Sub-Prior, Sacristan, Cellarer and Precentor of Holy Trinity Priory for refusing the accept him as the Visitor, the summons was annulled "by a higher authority". However, two years later the Pope, Innocènt IV, ordered the prior to accept, and admit, the archbishop to the priory—he did so! Many influential citizens gave the priory money in order to ensure a place for their burial and for a Mass to be said on the anniversary of their death every year. A Bishop of London was consecrated in the priory church, and the heart of John Peckham, Archbishop of Canterbury, 1279-1294, was also buried in the church. At one time the priory was given, by William of Ypres, the market by Queenhithe, on the condition that from their income they would give to the Hospital of St. Katherine by the

Tower the annual payment of twenty pounds. We are fortunate in being able to consult a plan of the priory made by a surveyor in the reign of Elizabeth I, 1558-1603, and in the archives of the Marquess of Salisbury at Hatfield House, Hertfordshire, and from it can be seen the great extent of the land occupied by the priory and its ancillary buildings. The plan is on two sheets which separately show the ground and the first floor plans, together with the City Wall, and the position of the parish church of St. Katharine Creechurch.

During the 12th and 13th centuries the house thrived to such a degree that it became one of the wealthiest in London, but its good fortune did not continue. In 1532 there was a general meeting of the Prior and Chapter of the house at which time they came to recognise that the income and property were diminishing, and that it was reduced by debts. They surrendered the house to the King, acting under the Suppression of the Monasteries Act of 1532. The site and buildings were acquired by Sir Thomas Audley who offered the church together with its fine peal of bells to the nearby parish of St. Katharine Creechurch. But the parishioners were unhappy at the prospect of accepting the offer, and the unfortunate new owner had to demolish the church building at his own great expense. Today all that is left above ground is one small arch from the church which has recently been incorporated into a new office building at the Aldgate end of Mitre Street.

Across the roadway from Mitre Street, at the junction of Aldgate, Leadenhall and Fenchurch Streets, stands the **Aldgate Pump** (10). Originally the pump was supplied by water from the nearby St. Michael's Well that stood hard by St. Michael's Church which had been taken down at the establishing of the Holy Trinity Priory here. Some years ago the water from the pump was analysed following comments that it tasted "different". During the course of the examination of the water the underground stream which fed the well was traced back to its source, and it was discovered that in its journey from the northern hills of London it passed, underground, through a cemetery and that the bones which had fallen into the stream were adding that "extra calcium taste to the water". The source was disconnected and now the water supply comes from the Thames Water Authority's reservoir! On the pump can be seen the brass head of a wolf which is said to commemorate the last one to be shot *in* the City of London—back in the 19th century.

Further along in Leadenhall Street on the corner with Creechurch Lane stands the **church of St. Katharine** (11).

The church stands on the site of at least two previous churches which formed part of the precinct of Aldgate Priory used by the laity of the priory and other local persons. The present church was consecrated in 1628 by the then Archbishop of Canterbury, William Laud, 1573-1645, who was beheaded on Tower Hill for his "Popish practices" when he upset the Puritans of the 17th century by using incense and praying in Latin. It was, however, the curate of the parish in the 16th century, one Sir Stephen by name, that has caught the eye, and pen, of the historian. He would preach from a high tree in the churchyard, sing High Mass in English from a tomb at the back of the church, and on one occasion so incited his congregation of the idolatry of worshipping Our Lady that they arose straight away and tore down the Maypole that used to hang under the eaves of the nearby church of St. Andrew Undershaft.

The **Parish Church of St. Andrew Undershaft** (12) is on the corner of Leadenhall Street and St. Mary Axe. Described as "an elegant specimen of the late pointed Gothic architecture" the present church dates from 1532, when it was rebuilt at the expense of several wealthy citizens. The suffix "Undershaft" refers to the Maypole (shaft) that was regularly used for May Day celebrations until the incident just referred to above, that of "Evil May Day" which caused the destruction of the shaft as being idolatrous. A nearby alley commemorates the maypole in its title Shaft Alley. One of the great heroes of the parish is undoubtedly John Stow, 1525-1605, whose "Survay of the City of London", first published in 1598, is a great source of information regarding the City in the Middle Ages and up to the time of its publication. Every year, usually the third Wednesday in April, the London and Middlesex Archaeological Society arranges for the Stow Service and Quill Ceremony to take place here. During the service a new quill is placed in the hand of John Stow's monument in the north east corner of the church, and an historian is asked to deliver a short address on some aspect of Stow and his times. Like its two neighbours, St. Katharine Creechurch, and St. Helen's Bishopsgate, St. Andrew Undershaft escaped destruction in the Great Fire of London in 1666, and received little damage in the Second World War, 1939-1945. On the door under the southwest corner tower can be seen a 16th century

sanctuary knocker, whose original purpose was to protect persons
fleeing from the law by granting them the sanctuary of the church—
if the church was closed they could hold on to the knocker and
thereby resist arrest. Also in the Middle Ages there stood in the parish of St. Andrew's the church of St. Mary Axe, which was closed in
1561 and the parish joined to that of St. Andrew Undershaft—the
full title of the former church being Our Lady, St. Ursula and the
Eleven Thousand Virgins.

At the far end of the street called St. Mary Axe, and at the junction
with Camomile Street there is a Corporation plaque marking the
site of the **"Papey"** (13).

Here stood the church of St. Augustine-super-murum, St. Augustine's on the Wall, which had been founded in 1170, and which in
1428 served only a handful of parishioners, and was annexed to the
Parish of All Hallows London Wall. However, in 1442 the Hospital,
or Hospice of Le Papey was founded by Thomas Symminsees, and
two other priests, it was intended for priests who because of their
age or infirmity were unable to carry out their full priestly duties in a
parish. The Founder, the local parish priest gave the now redundant
church of St. Augustine's to the hospice which was to continue until
the time of its Dissolution in the reign of Edward VI, 1547-1553. The
inhabitants were paid a small fee for attending and conducting
funeral services in the City. At the Dissolution the site was sold and
used for warehousing.

A short distance from the plaque can be seen a small garden which is
all that remains of the burial ground of St. Martin Outwich church
which once stood at the junction of Bishopsgate and Threadneedle
Street, also part of the site of the Papey in earlier days.

At the junction of Camomile Street and Bishopsgate turn left and
walk down Bishopsgate. Shortly will be found **Clark's Place** (14),
where the first hall of the Worshipful Company of Parish Clerks was
erected and where later an almshouse was to be found for those
members of the Company who became homeless at the suppression
of the Clerks in the 16th century.

A few yards further down Bishopsgate past Clark's Place is the
church of St. Ethelburga (15) which is first mentioned in 1278,
and rebuilt in the 14th century to provide a 'typical parish church of
medieval London' and one that has survived Great Fires, blitzes,
redundancies and redevelopments in the immediate vicinity.

Surely a great achievement for one so small a building! The patron saint of the parish St. Ethelburga, was the sister of St. Erconwald, Bishop of London from 675 to 685 A.D., who on his death was buried in the cathedral and whose shrine became highly popular in the Middle Ages. Ethelburga was the Abbes of Barking and the Founderess of the Parish Church of All Hallows by the Tower (Barking Church). Of all the rectors of the parish perhaps Blessed John Larke is most worthy of being mentioned. A friend of Saint Thomas More, who was able to help his friend by getting him appointed to the parish of Woodford, a great help since St. Ethelburga was a small parish with very limited financial resources. When he resigned from the living he was helped again by Saint Thomas More, and this time he was offered, and accepted the living of Chelsea, More's local parish church, and where he served as his personal chaplain. He left the City in 1542 but continued at Chelsea until 1544. By this time he had fallen foul of the Authority in refusing to submit to the supremacy of the King (Henry VIII) as head of the Church in England at that time. He was found guilty of treason, and hung, drawn and quartered at Tyburn on 7th March 1544. To commemorate the four hundredth anniversary of his martyrdom a plaque was erected in the church.

Further down Bishopsgate, and underneath a modern building's archway is Great St. Helen's Place and the **Parish Church of St. Helen.** (16). This is truly a remarkable building, incorporating as it does two churches joined together by a 16th century arcade of arches. Here was founded in the 11th century the parish church of St. Helen, the mother of the Roman Emperor Constantine the Great, c280-337 A.D., who himself was the first Emperor to become a Christian and to make Christianity the Faith of the Roman Empire. She has become particularly associated with the finding of the True Cross at Calvary in Jerusalem, several pieces of which can be found in London today. Alongside the parish church there was built in 1212 a Benedictine nunnery which was then incorporated in the parish church. So, here we have two naves and two chancels side by side, with a wall between that was taken down at the time of the Dissolution of the nunnery in the 16th century, to be replaced by the arcade of arches already mentioned. Within the Nun's Choir (Chancel) can be seen an Easter Sepulchre, the place where the Host was placed between Good Friday and Easter Day in Pre-English Reformation times. It probably owes its present day existence to the fact that for many years it was covered over and remained 'lost' until a restoration in the 19th century.

Under the Sepulchre can be seen an unusual 'squint' or 'hagioscope', with a number of small openings allowing persons outside the choir to see through the wall to the former High Altar and to be able to see the Host at the Elevation during the Mass. Opinions differ as to who was allowed to look into the church from this position. One school of thought is that it was the Infirmary of the nunnery and that the sick were thereby able to take part in the Mass, perhaps from their sick-beds. Across the people's choir can be seen the 14th century alabaster tombs of the Outwich family from the former parish church of St. Martin Outwich, pulled down in the 19th century to make way for offices. A Corporation plaque marks the spot at the Bishopsgate end of Threadneedle Street. The choir stall here came from the Nun's choir and the 15th century grotesque arm rests should be observed, in the area behind the organ there was, in medieval times two further chapels. The space is now used for offices. When the church was in need of repair in the early 17th century, Inigo Jones, the catholic architect, was employed by the parish to carry out the necessary restoration. The doorway on the south side of the church dates from this time, as does the font, and the inner porches of the church. The popular name for the church is the "Westminster Abbey of the City", borne out by the large number of monuments and tombs that can be found inside the church. Although the churchyard itself is small and very limited in content, inside the church lie buried Sir Thomas Gresham (died 1579) founder of the Royal Exchange, Sir Julius Caesar, a Master of the Rolls, (died in 1636), and a monumental brass to Thomas Wylliams and his wife who died in 1495, he is shown with a short Rosary hanging from his girdle. Sir John Crosby, d1475 also lies buried in the church—a great benefactor of the church and whose hall (house) stood nearby to the church.

Crosby Hall (17), the home of Sir John and Lady Crosby was built in the 15th century for Sir John who was a wealthy grocer and woolman of the City of London. After his death in 1475, the hall was let to Richard, Duke of Gloucester and it was here that he heard of the death of the two young princes in the Tower of London, (Edward V, 1470-1483, and his brother Richard, Duke of York), and that he was now the King of England. He ruled for only two years, being killed 21st August 1485 at the Battle of Bosworth Field, and was buried in the Greyfriars monastery in Leicester.

In the following century the hall was leased to Saint Thomas More, but there is no direct evidence that he lived there for any length of time, probably only during the time that he was waiting for "The Great House" at Chelsea to reach completion. Later Saint Thomas More's son-in-law, William Roper who had married Margaret More, lived in the hall. All except the hall of the mansion was destroyed in the Great Fire of London in 1666.

From St. Helen's church and the site of Crosby Hall it is a short walk to the cross-roadways of Bishopsgate-Cornhill-Gracechurch Street and Leadenhall Street, at which junction there stood **"The Standard upon Cornhill"** (18) until 1674 when it was removed. From here were measured distances to and from London, the original stone being a Roman Milestone or Millestone, a mile being a mille or one thousand paces of a Roman soldier. It is also thought that "London Stone", which now resides in the wall of a bank in Cannon Street, was to be placed here, and that it had some 'magical powers'. Shakespeare in Henry VI, Part Two, has Jack Cade, the rebel leader, strike the stone with his sword and declare "Mortimer is now Lord of the City".

Walk down Gracechurch Street to Fenchurch Street and turn left, walking along until Mark Lane is reached, walk down the lane, past the tower of the former church of **All Hallows Staining** (19), which Stow claims was so-called from the fact the it was built of stone, he goes on to say the staining comes from the fact that the Painter Stainers, one of the Livery Companies of the City, had members of the Company living here.

Turn left along Hart Street to the **Parish Church of St. Olave** (20). Dedicated to St. Olaf, King of Norway, 995-1030, the church is shown in earlier records as being "S. Olave juxta Turrim", i.e. "St. Olave near the Tower (of London)". The first mention of the church was in the 13th century, although the church is thought to have existed in Pre-Conquest—1066 and all that—times when it would have been a wooden structure. All that remains of the 13th century church today is the crypt chapel underneath the tower—above ground the church was rebuilt in the 15th century and fully restored after extensive bomb damage in the Second World War, 1939-1945.

There are a number of interesting monuments in the church, the most ancient of which is a tablet on the east wall of the south aisle to Doctor William Turner. In addition to being the Dean of Wells, was also the physician to the Protector Somerset, and he produced the botanical book, "Herbal", the first of its kind to be published in English in the 16th century.

From the church it is a short walk back to Tower Hill underground station from where the walk began.

Parish Church of St Andrew Undershaft

Cheapside—medieval marketplace

1 St. Paul's Underground station (Central Line)
2 British Telecom Building
3 Panyer Alley
4 St. Martin le Grand—'blue-plaque'
5 Aldersgate—'blue-plaque'
6 St. Botolph's church
7 Plaisterers' Hall
8 Noble Street—city wall
9 St. Anne and St. Agnes church
10 Goldsmiths' Hall
11 Wax Chandlers' Hall
12 St. Alban's tower
13 Parish Clerks Company Hall—site of
14 St. Mary Aldermanbury church site
15 Guildhall
16 St. Lawrence Jewry church
17 Mercers Company Hall
18 Thomas Becket's birthplace—'blue-plaque'
19 St. Mary Le Bow church
20 Bow Lane
21 "The Standard" in Cheapside
22 Milk Street
23 Mitre Court
24 Wood Street compter
25 St. Peter's Wood Street—church site
26 Eleanor Cross—site of
27 Shops in Cheapside
28 St. Vedast Foster Lane church
29 Corner of Cheapside
30 St. Paul's Cathedral

Cheapside—medieval marketplace

Our walk begins from **St. Paul's underground** station (1) where the busy streets of the City of London meet at the junction of St. Martin le Grand, Cheapside and Newgate Street. It will take us along the street that in medieval times was the main market of the city—Cheapside, to some of the interesting side streets thereabout. Many of the side streets recall the goods that were sold there in the Middle Ages, such as Bread Street, Friday Street (the scene of the Friday Fish Market), Wood Street, Milk Street and Honey Lane, added to which certain portions of the Chepe itself was alloted to specific goods.

Originally the street was called Crown after the inn which stood there, and then, later, West Chepe (as opposed to East Chepe, that is still to be found leading to the Tower of London), both taking their names from the Saxon word 'chepe', to barter or exchange. The street was once the widest street in the City of London and was often used for pageants, tournaments and other festive occasions. Opposite the underground station stands the **British Telecom** offices (2), opened in 1985, with its double atrium in the centre of the building making an impressive sight. It is built over the site of the Priory of St. Martin Le Grand, and the parish church of St. Nicholas Shambles where in 1138 a grammar school was founded. The Collegiate Church of St. Martin Le Grand was founded according to tradition by Winithred, King of Kent from 694 to 725 A.D., and served by an Order of Secular Canons until 1498 when Henry VII, 1457-1509, gave the priory to the Abbey of St. Peter at Westminster. It had become a royal chapel at the time of William the Conqueror, 1027-1087, in 1086 and by the terms of the Royal Charter enjoyed exemption from ecclesiastical and civic jurisdiction, with all the rights of sanctuary. It survived as a sanctuary until 1815 when the Act of Parliament authorising it was abolished, and the General Post Office erected their own building on the site. Excavations in the 19th century revealed the foundations of the church, which were two hundred feet in length, a vault of Edward III's, 1312-1377, time, and the remains of a Roman villa that once stood on the site. When the present building was being erected the remains of the medieval church of St. Nicholas in the Shambles was revealed for the first time for four hundred years. The church was demolished when the church of the former Greyfriars Monastery was made into the parish church—this was at the time of the English Reformation of the 16th century. The church of St. Nicholas was founded before 1291, and served the "Shambles" the medieval meat market of the City. In the recent excavations a number of skeletons were unearthed including one of a pregnant woman who had died before the child was born. The baby's skeleton was resting in the pelvis of its mother, this and all the other bones were carefully recorded by the archaeologists. Before leaving the immediate area of the underground station, turn left, and find the **Panyer Steps** (3) with the Panyer Boy. The verse below the carved figure of the panyer boy, the boy who delivered bread in the City and used a panyer (bread-basket) to help him carry his goods, reads:-

"When ye have sought the citie round, yet still this is
the highest ground"

Regretfully this is not true. Cornhill is several inches higher than Ludgate Hill where St. Paul's Cathedral stands. Return to the station and cross the roadway and walk along St. Martin le Grand, noting the **"blue-plaque"** (4) on the wall of one of the buildings. Walk along the right hand side footpath of the street. Cross Gresham Street, and shortly after the Lord Raglan Public House can be seen another "blue-plaque". This time it commemorates the site of **Aldersgate** (5), one of the older gateways into the City of London. It is first mentioned in the 13th century as Ealdredsgate, implying that a family by that name either built the gate or rebuilt it at that time. Stow refers to it as being the elder- or older- gate of the city. It is known to have existed in the time of the Roman occupation when it was the north gate of Londinium. The medieval gate was replaced in 1617 by a handsome building, three storeys high, with towers on each of the corners. On the outer side of the gate there was a statue of James VI of Scotland, 1566-1625, who in 1603 became James I of England, as well as retaining the Kingdom of Scotland. And so began the unification of England and Scotland, which with the Principality of Wales make up the United Kingdom of Great Britain. It was through this gateway that the King rode to claim the throne of England after the death in 1603 of Elizabeth I, 1533-1603. With the advent of gunpowder both the City Wall and its Gates were obsolete and eventually in the 18th century the gates were all demolished. But not before John Day had used Aldersgate for his printing works, and had had the gate painted on the side of his personal coach.

Just beyond the site of the gate stands the **Guild Church of St. Botolph's Aldersgate** (6). The church and churchyard stand just outside the City Wall, and the first mention of a parish is in 1260 when the patrons of the benefice were the Canons of the nearby St. Martin's Priory. Later in the reign of Henry VII, 1457-1509, the patronage passed to the Dean and Chapter of Westminster Abbey. Today's patron is the Bishop of London. The first recorded rector of the parish was John de Steventon in 1333, while the churchwardens' account and the parochial records date from 1466.

Stow mentions in his "Survay" that in 1377 the Brotherhood of St. Fabian and St. Sebastian was founded in the church, and another in 1446 in honour of the Holy Trinity. This latter Brotherhood was endowed with lands worth more than thirty pounds a year, by Dame Joan Astley to 'Perpetually have a master and two custodians, with brethren and sisters'. It was finally dissolved at the time of Edward VI, 1537-1553. In the Chronicle of the Greyfriars there is recorded a strange story of medieval sacrilege:-

"This yere (1532) . . . the sacrament at sent Butteles at Aldersgate on Good Friday in the mornynge was stolne owte at the est wyndow and iij ostess wrappyd in a rede clothe and a woman browte it unto the porter of the Gray freeres and she tane and broote unto the shreffe". Although the medieval church survived the Great Fire of London (1666) the building fell into a ruinous state and had to be rebuilt during the latter half of the 18th century. There are some monuments from the old church preserved in the present building, and include Dame Anne Packington d. 1563, who founded a set of almshouses in the grounds of the former White Friars precinct off Fleet Street, Sir John Micklethwaite, d. 1683, physician to

Charles II, who was President of the Royal College of Physicians. A celebrated bookseller/publisher of the 17th and 18th century, Richard Chiswell, was born in the parish and became an important benefactor to it, and is commemorated in an ornamental tablet. He died in 1711. In 1893 the churchyard was excavated and all the human remains were transferred to Brookwood, near Woking in Surrey, in the London Necroplis Company cemetery grounds and an obelisk erected. An inscription reads "to the memory of generations of parishioners formerly buried in the church of St. Botolph, Aldersgate". It was then that the coffin of Richard Chiswell was discovered covered with a marble stone, which can now be seen inside the church at the doorway leading to the churchyard. An 18th century painted window fills the east wall of the church in which the artist James Pearson, shows the "Agony of Christ in the Garden of Gethesmane". All the glass in the south aisle of the church is modern replacing glass that was destroyed in the Second World War, 1939-1945, and is the work of M.C. Farrar-Bell. The theme of these windows is the history of the church and the immediate surrounding area.

Until recent developments off Aldersgate there existed a Trinity Court, opposite where the Museum of London now stands, and was so-called after the Brotherhood of the Holy Trinity founded here in the parish in 1377. They are not to be confused with the Friars of the Holy Trinity, or "Maturines" as they were sometimes known after their mother house near St. Maturines in Paris, whose work was the redemption of captives. This, however, would not have been inappropriate in the 20th century the parish being at one time the home of the Rehabilitation of Discharged Prisoners.

The Brotherhood, or Guild, had been founded in 1373 in honour of the Blessed Sacrament, part of their duties being to maintain thirteen candles made of wax, around the Easter Sepulchre at St. Botolph's. On Trinity Sunday their chaplain celebrated Mass in honour of the Blessed Sacrament and of the Holy Trinity, and they "made their offerings". In the church itself they had their own window which showed a significant symbol of the Trinity.

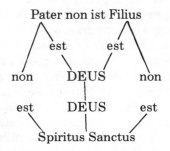

This famous definition of the Holy and Undivided Trinity also formed a banner for Henry V, 1387-1422, and was carried before him in battle—notably at Agincourt.

In addition to helping the parish priest, the chaplain was also bound to say Mass every morning, winter and summer alike, at 5 a.m. making a special mention, before Mass, of the Holy Trinity. On the Sunday after All Souls' Day, 2nd November, he would read out the names of the departed brothers and sisters of the Guild, from the pulpit of the church.

After visiting the church return to the east end of the building and enter the churchyard by the wrought iron gateway on the south side. On the left hand side, can be seen the memorial plaque to John and Charles Wesley, the founders of the Methodist Church, whose 'conversion' is said to have taken place in a nearby house in the 18th century. The churchyard is more commonly known as the "Postmen's Park", due to its closeness to the General Post Office in King Edward Street, and for the fact that the Post Office Workers' Union have permission to hold union meetings there if they so wish. Standing on a mound of earth in the churchyard is the figure of "The Minotaur", by Michael Ayrton, 1921-1975, which is one of two sculptures by him in the City of London, the other being Icarus, near St. Nicholas Cole Abbey church. Both were erected in 1973. Within the confines of the churchyard can also be found the Geo. Fred. Watts Memorial Cloisters where the everyday deeds of heroism are recorded by means of ceramic plaques. George Frederick Watts, 1817-1904, conceived the idea, which he hoped would spread to other cities throughout the country, of recording for posterity the many deeds of heroism when persons remembered lost their lives saving

another's. Having saved three children in a fire in the Borough, in
Southwark, Alice Ayres lost her life trying to save a fourth. The railway worker who threw a fellow worker out of the way of an oncoming
train, and was killed himself. The small statue of G.F. Watts in the
cloister was carved by T.H. Wren, and bears the inscription "The
utmost for the highest". There are fifty-three plaques in total of
which thirteen were erected by Watts himself and the remainder by
his widow. In August 1987 there was privately published by H.
Dagnall a booklet on these memorials, which is available from him
at 30 Turner Road, Queensbury, Edgware, Middx, HA8 6AY.

Leave the churchyard by the gateway in St. Martin-Le-Grand, and
crossing the roadway turn right into London Wall.

Here can be found the **Worshipful Company of Plaisterers's
Hall** (7). The Company, an important craft guild, was first mentioned in the 14th century in the City archives, although it did not
receive its Charter until the time of Henry VII, 1485-1509. The Company a founder member of the City & Guilds Institute, still main-
tains an active interest in the making and using of plaster, through
the many competitions, for which it presents prizes at the Technical
Colleges in London. In an attempt to prevent bad workmanship
after the Great Fire of London in 1666, the Charter of the Company
was further extended to encompass an area of three miles distant
from the City of London. Under the same edict no man was allowed
to carry on the trades of mason, bricklayer or plaisterer at the same
time who was not a guild member. Right up to the early 19th century
the Company exercised its power of search to visit the premises of
its members and to control of the work standards. The coat of arms
of the Company can be seen on the outside wall of the hall, and
shows the motto "Let brotherley love continue", the tools of the
trade, the Red Rose of England supported on either side by the
fleur-de-lis of Our Lady, the saintly patron of the guild.

To the side of the hall runs Noble Street, with several stretches of
the **City Wall** (8) visible along the route of the roadway. Here in the
17th century lived Robert Tichbourne, Lord Mayor of London in
1656, and a signatory on the death warrant for Charles I, 1600-1649.
In the 1322 "Calendar of Coroners of London" there appears the
name of Thomas le Noble owning land here and giving it to the
street. In the street can be seen the Plaisterers Silver Jubilee Garden, designed to commemorate Her Majesty the Queen's Silver

Jubilee in 1977. The site is edged by the remains of the Roman and Medieval City Wall. It was formally opened by the late Dean of St. Paul's cathedral, the Very Rev. Martin Sullivan.

At the end of Noble Street where it joins to Gresham Street, named after the famous 16th century family whose members included Sir Thomas Gresham the founder of Gresham's Bank, and of the Royal Exchange, stands the **Parish Church of St. Anne and St. Agnes** (9). This was formerly known as St. Anne-by-the-Willows from the trees which, lined a nearby street. Today the church serves the congregation of the Lutheran Church. The church was founded circa 1137 and after its destruction in the Great Fire of London in 1666 was rebuilt by Sir Christopher Wren. It was bombed in the Second World War, 1939-1945, and has since been faithfully restored to Wren's original designs. In an inventory taken in 1250 the parish is recorded as owning one Chalice, a Breviary, two sets of fine vestments, and a silken banner. At a later time there were added to the list two tankards one of which had the curious inscription:-

"This pott for holy wine,
This wine pure blood,
This blood true life,
This life contains all good
Not potts, but souls are fil to hold such wine,
Such blood, such life, such good
Oh Christ take mine"

and the other:-

"My saviour by an art divine,
Conveighs his blood to me in wine,
Faith spies the secret, and reveals
As much to love, love closely steals
My heart unto this pott where graven
This stood
This for thy wine sweet Lord, this for thy blood"

During the 16th century the Puritans destroyed the beauty of many of the churches throughout the country, and none more so than here at St. Anne and St. Agnes. The entire interior was white-washed and all traces of the medieval paintings on the walls extinguished. Here even the font was removed and a 'basin' brought in to replace it during the administration of Holy Baptism. At least two of the incumbents of the parish died for their beliefs. The Reverend Love was beheaded after he had protested at the execution of Charles I, 1600-1649, and John Claydon was burnt at Smithfield for his beliefs in 1415. Also in the 15th century William Gregory, Lord Mayor in 1451, founded a chantry here, and was buried in it. The churchyard and the adjoining open space have now been dedicated to the public and are maintained by the Corporation of the City of London.

On the opposite corner to the church at the end of Vedast Lane stands the Hall of the **Worshipful Company of Goldsmiths** of the City of London (10). The Fraternity or Guild of Goldsmiths is recorded as being in existence in the 12th century. The Company received its first Charter in 1327, while in 1462 they were granted their corporate title "The Wardens and Commonalty of the Mystery of Goldsmiths of the City of London". In the rooms attached to the hall can be seen many splendid examples of the work of the craftsmen of the Company. Among their many duties of maintaining the highest of standards in their craft is that of testing the coinage of the Realm. This takes place in February each year at the Trial of the Pyx when, under the various Coinage Acts, coins from the Royal Mint that have been set aside are brought to the hall and tested. The present Hall was designed by Philip Hardwick, 1792-1870, and completed by 1835. Although the French goldsmiths adopted St. Eligius, born near Limoges c. 588 A.D. and died at Noyon in 660 A.D., whose feast day is the 1st December, the Goldsmiths of London adopted St. Dunstan as their patron who is accredited with dexterity as a metalworker and bell founder. Dunstan born near Glastonbury c. 909 and died at Canterbury in 988 A.D., whose feast day, 19th May, is still honoured by the Company today. In the medieval hall there was a silver-gilt image of St. Dunstan, and in the nearby church of St. John Zachary, now an open space in Gresham Street, a candle was kept burning in honour of the saint.

On the vigil of St. Dunstan the Wardens and Court of Assistants, preceded by their four chaplains, would process to St. Paul's Cathedral to the chapel dedicated to St. Dunstan to take part in the service prior to the election of a new Master for the Company. On the feast day itself, after dinner, the whole Livery went to the cathedral to the 'general obit and dirge' for all the brethren and sisters of the company. In the latter part of the 14th century the Wardens and the Dean and Chapter of St. Paul's Cathedral entered into an agreement whereby the Guild were responsible for the upkeep of the

Chapel of St. Dunstan in the cathedral, as a chantry chapel to John Hyltoft who had bequeathed ample funds to the Company for this purpose.

The **Worshipful Company of Wax Chandlers's** hall (11) is on the corner of Gutter Lane and Gresham Street, and is first mentioned in the 14th century when Ordinances were given for the government of the craft of wax chandlers. These were the craftsmen who made candles and tapers from good wax (of bees) unmixed with fat or other adulterants. Much of the produce of this Company was used by the church and the great households whereas the Tallow Chandlers' wares were used for domestic and street lighting. The wax chandlers' raw material was beeswax that had been purified and bleached. The Company once had jurisdiction over the making of candles in the City and within ten miles of its wall. Their motto is "Truth is the Light". From the hall it is a short walk to Wood Street, and the sole remains of **St. Alban's church—a tower** (12).

Built originally as a chapel by King Offa, d 796 A.D., for the nearby royal palace and dedicated to the pro-martyr of England—S. Alban who was executed at Verulamium (now part of the modern City of St. Albans), in the 3rd century. Little is known of the saint save for the fact (?) that he was a Romano-Briton living here during the time of persecution of Christians by the Romans. Alban was said to have been found guilty of harbouring a Christian who converted him to the Christian Faith and later they were both executed. Depending on which Kalendar is used his feast day is 22nd or 17th June. The church fell into disrepair in the 17th century and was rebuilt by Inigo Jones, 1573-1652, and only the tower remains. In 1985 this was converted into living and office quarters with a roof garden.

From the church tower it is a short walk to the City Corporation's "blue-plaque" marking the site of the third, and last, Hall of the **Worshipful Company of Parish Clerks** of the City of London (13). One of the oldest Companies of the City its members represent one hundred and fifty churches that can be found in and around the City. Not strictly a Livery Company—the Lord Mayor and Corporation does not recognise their cassock and surplice as being 'livery'. But the Company continues to serve both Church and State faithfully as it has for nigh on one thousand years. In the past members have been responsible for the compiling, printing and publishing the Bills of Mortality, which listed the number of deaths, etc., in each parish in their charge, as well as undertaking other parochial duties such as teaching Sunday School, and helping to the incumbent in the daily offices of the church.

From the plaque it is a short walk to the site of the church of **St. Mary Aldermanbury** (14). First recorded in 1181, the medieval church was burnt down in the Great Fire of 1666, and rebuilt by Sir Christopher Wren whose building was gutted by fire in the Second World War, 1939-1945, the ruins of which were presented to Westminster College, in Fulton, Missouri, U.S.A. The building has been re-erected there and commemorates Sir Winston Churchill's 1874-1965, famous "Iron Curtain" speech there in 1946. One of a select number of Lord Mayors of London, William Estfield twice held office, in 1429 and 1437, and was a benefactor of the church in the 15th century—according to Stow, he built the steeples, and gave five tunable bells and one hundred pounds. He also founded a chantry here and was buried in it. Stow records that in the cloisters of the church there could be seen a shank bone of a man that was larger, by three and a half inches, to the one that could seen in nearby St. Lawrence Jewry. The parish records show that foundlings in the parish were given the surname "Aldermanbury", or "Berry" for short, the register of 1586 having an entry citing that the Beadle was paid, six days a week, to "seeke for the Mother of a child which was left in the parish". To-day the foundations of the church that are left make up part of a very pleasant garden area.

A short walk from the 'garden-church' can be found the **Guildhall** of the City of London (15) from which place the City is governed. The medieval Hall, built between 1411 and 1425, the porch being added in 1430, as was also the Guildhall Chapel added to the right of the porch. The chapel dedicated to Our Lady, St. Mary Magdalene and All Saints survived until 1782 when it was demolished following the decision to use the nearby church of St. Lawrence Jewry instead, at which time the building was used as a court room. The chapel had been founded in 1368 by three citizens, Adam, Francis and Henry de Frowick who provided for a warden, seven priests, three clerks, and four choristers. Later in 1417 the College of Priests was confiscated by the Corporation because of the lax behaviour of the inhabitants.

The Great Hall was also used for famous trials it being the largest hall in England, after the great hall at Westminster, with Anne

Askew was tried for heresy here in 1546, "she spoke against the sacrament of the altar", i.e. transubstantiation, for which she was put on the rack several times until she lost the use of her limbs. Twice she recanted but was finally burnt at the stake in Smithfield, having been carried there in a wooden chair, "she being too weak to walk". Brought to trial on the 29th March 1606 here was Father Henry Garnet, Superior of the English Jesuits, he was found guilty and executed in St. Paul's churchyard, having been imprisoned in the Tower of London for five weeks after his trial, on 3rd May 1606—the Feast day of the Invention of the Cross. When he arrived at the place of his execution he made the sign of the Cross, and recited, "In nomine Patris et Filii et Spiritus Sancti. Adoramus te, Christe, et benedicamus tibi, quia per sanctam crucem tuam redemisti mundum" "In the name of the Father, and of the Son and of the Holy Spirit. We adore Thee O Christ, and we bless thee, because by Thy Holy Cross Thou hast redeemed the world". He repeated these and other such phrases three times, and then told the hangman he was ready. The Hall was also the scene of the trial of Thomas Cranmer, Archbishop of Canterbury, 1533-1556, who was appointed to the Arch-Diocese by Henry VIII, 1491-1547, for his support in the conflict with the Pope, Clement VII, 1478-1534, over his claim for an annulment. In 1533 Cranmer annulled the marriage and accepted Henry VIII as the Supreme Head of the Church of England. Cranmer was a prime mover in the English Reformation, but on the accession to the throne of Mary was condemned as a heretic and burnt at the stake in Oxford where today there stands the Martyrs Memorial Cross. High up on the roof line of the Hall can be seen the many shields depicting the coats of arms of the Livery Companies of the City of London, many of whom were founded in the Middle Ages.

Across the Guildhall Yard can be found the Guild **Church of St. Lawrence Jewry** (16), with its curiously shaped weather-vane bearing the grid-iron symbol on which the saint was martyred. He was one of the seven deacons of Rome in the 3rd century who, when ordered to produce his church's treasures lined up all the poor and needy of his parish. Tradition records that he was roasted alive on a grid-iron on the site where the church of St. Lawrence-without-the-walls stands today in Rome, where he is revered as that city's third patron saint. Founded in the 12th century, the church was destroyed in the Great Fire of 1666, and again in the Second World War, 1939-1945. The church which has been "repaired and sumptuously furnished", largely at the cost of the Corporation of London, is today the Guild Church of the Corporation, and is used regularly by the Lord Mayor for services. Since the demolition of the Guildhall Chapel services held prior to the election of a Lord Mayor are held here. In the Pre-Fire church were buried the great-grandfather of Anne Boleyn, the second 'wife' of Henry VIII, and the father of Sir Thomas Gresham, the founder of the Royal Exchange in the 16th century. The stained glass windows of the church show, amongst other noted persons, the likeness of Saint Thomas More, 1478-1535, who was born in nearby Milk Street, and who delivered a public lecture here on the subject of "S. Augustine de civitate"—a privilege accorded to only a few distinguished academic layman in the 16th century.

A short walk from the church, along Gresham Street is Ironmonger Lane, at the end of which can be seen the Hall of the **Worshipful Company of Mercers** of the City of London (17). The Company received its first Ordinances, rules under which the Companies operate, in 1347, and their first Royal Charter, was granted in 1394, with later Charters being given in 1425, and 1559. Only the last Charter still exists today in the archives of the Company. The Company takes its name from the French word "mercier" which means a dealer, trader, in small ware—they exported wool and woollen cloth and imported linen, fine silks and velvets in exchange. Included in the famous liverymen of the past are such names as Saint Thomas More, Sir Thomas Seymour, "Dick" Whittington, and more recently Lord Baden Powell, founder of the Boy Scout Movement. On the site of the Hall was the house of Gilbert Becket, a Mercer and a Portreeve of London, and the father of Saint Thomas Becket, Archbishop of Canterbury, 1118-1170. The saint was born here, a Corporation **plaque** (18) in Cheapside records the fact, and this was also the site of the Hospital of St. Thomas of Acon, the latter having been founded by Thomas's sister, Agnes, on the death of her brother. At the time of the English Reformation and the Dissolution of the Monasteries in the 16th century the site was sold to the Mercers' Company who have occupied the site ever since that time. Within the Company's building there is a small chapel, a very popular place of worship in Post-Reformation times when it became well known for the sermons, preached in Italian and Spanish for the benefit of Protestants from those countries. In the aftermath of the destruction of the Second World War workmen found, buried in the floor of the chapel, a 16th century figure of Christ laying in soft earth two feet below the surface. It appears to have been a Pieta, and was buried for safety at the time of the Reformation. For access to the Hall it is advisable to contact the City Information Centre, St. Paul's Churchyard, E.C.4. when guided tours are arranged during the summer months for various Company Halls in the City. From the Mercers' Hall it is a short walk, along Cheapside to the **Parish Church of St. Mary Le Bow**. (19)

It was in 1077 that the original, Saxon, church was badly damaged by fire and had to be rebuilt by the Normans in 1087. The New St. Mary's church, to distinguish it from the nearby St. Mary Aldermary ("older-Mary") church, was built over the bows, or arches of the earlier building, and so became known, in time, as S. Mary de Arcubus, or St. Mary Le Bow. The arches to be found in the crypt of the church are still in a good state of repair, and are the place where the Court of the Arches meets from time to time. The Court is the Supreme Court of the Church of England, where, for example all bishops of the Church have their appointments confirmed by the Court. It was here too that Cardinal Pole, the last Catholic Archbishop of Canterbury came in 1556 shortly after he had arrived in England. He was dedicated in Bow Church, where, rich in costly robes and sitting on a guilded throne, his Pall was presented to him. Adorned therewith, Pole presently mounts the pulpit and makes a "drie sermon of the use and honour of the Pall" records Fuller in his Church History, published in 1645. The bells of the church are world famous it being said that anybody born within the sound of them can claim to be a Cockney.

The Medieval church's bells were also used to ring the Curfew each evening. Early in the reign of William the Conqueror, 1027-1087, it was decreed that each night certain church bells should ring out at 9 o'clock and that that should be the signal for all citizens to cover their fires in preparation for going to bed. Fire being a constant hazard in the history of the City of London it was essential that it be extinguished completely before the family retired for the night. In the morning the reverse happened and the bell acted as an alarm clock for the apprentices and their masters to be roused from their sleep to begin the day's work. However, all was not well at times in the City and an early example of wall-graffiti appeared on the side of the church which ran:-

"Clarke of the Bow Bell with the yellow locks,
For thy late ringing they head shall have knockes"
   to which the clerk responded:-
"Children of Cheape, hold you all still,
For you shall have the Bow Bell rung at your will"

On his death John Donne, Dean of St. Paul's, c1572-1631, left money in his will for the maintenance of the Great Bell of Bow. It was in 1271 that the bell-tower of the church crashed to the ground in Cheapside killing a number of people. Later when it was rebuilt, after the style of Wren's steeple for St. Dunstan in the East, five lanterns were incorporated into the design of the tower. At night lights burned on the tower which served as a guide to travellers coming into the City. This tower is shown on the medieval seal of the church. According to another rhyme it was the bells from this church that told the young "Dick" Whittington to "turn again" on Highgate Hill in North London, as he rested on his way back to his country home in Gloucestershire. Today the spot is marked with a memorial that also includes the legendary cat. The balcony on the Cheapside frontage of the church was placed there in memory of the earlier ones from which kings and queens of England would watch the tournaments and pageants in the street below. Although Wren replaced the balcony after the Great Fire it has never been used for its intended purpose. Charles II, 1630-1685, was to have watched the Lord Mayor's procession from it, but, on hearing that there was a plot to assassinate both him and his brother, the Duke of York, if they stood there, they watched the procession from another safer place in the City. In Edward III's, 1313-1377, time the wooden balcony collapsed, injuring several people. The king was so enraged that he immediately ordered the hanging of the carpenter responsible for the work. But his queen, Phillipa of Hainault, 1312-1369, is recorded as having pleaded for him on her bended knees, and his life was spared. But this event of the 14th century does not bear comparison with the dreadful happening in 1284 when a murder was committed in the tower of the church. In a fight at the cathedral end of Cheapside a goldsmith by the name of Duckett seriously injured a man named Crispin, and then took refuge in the church tower where friends of the injured man found him, and killed him. All would have been well for them except that a young boy was at the time hiding in the tower, and saw the men although they tried to make it look like suicide, on the evidence of the boy they were convicted of murder. As a result of the incident sixteen people were executed, including one woman. The church was closed and an interdict, (an ecclesiastical censure), placed on the parish. This forbids the celebration of the Mass and deprives the recipients from receiving other Sacraments until the order has been lifted. The earliest recorded Interdict was in the 6th century when, as in later times of the Middle ages, Popes would use the Order against offending Kings and Emperors. Whole countries would be placed under the Order possibly for offences committed by the rulers and not the people of the country. It was one of the most powerful devices ever used by the Church, it can still be used today. As recently as 1929 an American bishop issued an Interdict on a parish in his diocese for refusing to accept a coloured priest that he had himself had appointed. It is not recorded how long the Order lasted in the parish of St. Mary Le Bow.

In **Bow Lane** (20) which runs alongside the east wall of the church there was a Catholic Chapel from 1809 to 1859 which was dedicated to St. Thomas the Apostle probably taking its dedication from the former parish church of St. Thomas the Apostle nearby that had been destroyed in the great Fire of 1666 and not rebuilt afterwards. John Stow in his "Survay of the City of London" records that the Mayor of London, one John Barnes, or Bernes, left to the former parish a chest and 1000 marks to be lent to some young man "upon sufficient pawne", and for the use thereof to say "De Profundis" or "Pater Noster", and no more". The chapel was served either by German or Polish priests living in London, and on its closure the congregation moved to Whitechapel. A school for Catholics was attached to the chapel with Father Francis Muth a Jesuit acting as the teacher, and where Father Edward Scott, S.J. who was the Procurator and Bursar for the English Province also served in the Chapel.

Return to Cheapside once more and cross the roadway, turn left and walk away from the church, past Honey Lane, and then shortly afterwards pause—here in the centre of the roadway stood the **Standard of Cheapside** (21).

Here punishments were carried out such as the three men who helped a prisoner escape in 1293 (their right hands were cut off,) and there are frequent mentions in the records of seditious books being burnt, and other offending goods being destroyed. The new Lord Mayor having taken his Oath of Allegiance to the Monarch would be accompanied by Master and Wardens of his Livery Company, together with the Sergeant of Arms, Mace Bearer, and Sword-bearer going in front, with a Sheriff on either side, and the City Recorder with the Aldermen in due order would walk down "The Cheape" and pause at "The Standard" so that all might recognise the new Lord Mayor. An unruly mob in 1326 took upon themselves to murder the then Bishop of Exeter, Walter de Stapledon. He had served Clement V, 1305-1320 (who established a Papal Residence at Avignon where it remained for seventy years), as his chaplain, and later became the Professor of Canon Law at the University of Oxford. But it was while carrying out his duties as Treasurer to Edward II, 1284-1327, that he incurred the hatred of the citizens of London. Having taken the law into their own hands they beheaded him "at the Standard in Chepe". Even "The Standard" itself did not escape the wrath of some of the inhabitants of London during the reign of Henry VI, 1421-1471, who ascended to the Throne in 1422 at the somewhat tender age of nine months, and within two months was also King of France, on the death of Charles VI, his maternal grandfather, 1380-1422. A serious quarrel was started between the men of the Cordwainer Ward and those of the Bread Street Ward as to which of them had the right to erect a shed near "The Standard" from which the frequent entertainments could be viewed. As the construction was on the south side of "The Standard" it was deemed to be in the former's jurisdiction. There is no clear indication as to when "The Standard" was actually first erected in The Chepe, but in 1442, Henry VI, 1421-1471, was petitioned and granted a licence for its repair. It consisted of a tall column of stone, with sculptures on each of six sides, and was surmounted by a figure of a man blowing a trumpet. In addition executions were carried out here by Wat Tyler and Jack Cade in 1450, who had Lord Saye, the Lord Treasurer beheaded here. On gala days "The Standard" was decked out with flowers, etc., and was 'dressed fayre agaynste the tyme', and at its foot 'was placed a noyse of trumpettes with baners and furniture', and all this to welcome Elizabeth I, 1533-1603, as she passed through the City on her way to her Coronation at Westminster Abbey. After the Great Fire of 1666 the ruins of "The Standard" were removed as an impediment to the traffic.

Leave the site of "The Standard", and walking towards St. Paul's Cathedral here one leaves the Ward of Cheapside and enters that of Bread Street.

Here on the north side of the street is **Milk Street** (22), where Saint Thomas More was born on the 7th February, 1478 "between the second and third hour of the morning". There is no plaque marking the site of the house.

Mitre Court (23) is to found off Milk Street where in the centre of the courtyard can be seen a canopy over a short flight of steps that led down to the remains of the **Wood Street Compter** (24). Here were imprisoned many Catholics during the 16th century. It was opened as a prison in September 1555 replacing an older one in nearby Bread Street. In April 1581 Saint Alexander Briant, a seminary Jesuit priest, born in the West Country in 1553 and educated at Hart College, Oxford, was condemned on a fictitious charge of plotting in Rome and in Belgium. He was later taken to Tyburn where he was "hung, drawn and quartered", on the 1st December, but not before he had been 'racked and pricked' in the Tower of London in an attempt to force him to disclose the whereabouts of Father Person. In 1586 Blessed Robert Dibdale was also incarcerated in the compter. Born in Warwickshire in 1558 he studied at Douai, before going to Rheims to be ordained in 1584. He was arrested in London together with Blessed John Lowe, both Londoners and priests by vocation, the latter having been ordained in Rome in 1582. Blessed Robert Dibdale's other companion arrested with him was Blessed John Adams a seminary priest from Winterbourne in Dorset. He had on three other occasions managed to escape but this time he failed to do so. All three were "hung, drawn and quartered" at Tyburn on 8th October 1586. Among the many other Catholics imprisoned here was Saint Ann Lyne, or Line, who was hung at Tyburn, 27th February 1601. She was found to be guilty of harbouring a priest. Her husband, Roger had been arrested in Bishopsgate St. Without with her and her brother, William Heigham, while attending Mass. Both her husband and brother escaped death and made their way to the Continent where they died of natural causes. At the same time that Saint Ann Lyne was hung at Tyburn, Saint Roger Filcock, a Jesuit Priest and Saint Mark Barkworth, a Benedictine monk, were both "hung, drawn and quartered" for being priests of the Catholic Church. On her arrival at Tyburn Saint Ann Lyne kissed the gallows, and kneeling down, began her prayers. She continued praying until her life was ended. In January 1586 Blessed William Thompson, a seminary priest, was brought to the Wood Street Compter, and after a short trial found guilty of being a priest, taken to Tyburn, in April that year, and "hung, drawn and quartered".

Through the archway near the "Hole in the Wall" public house can be found Wood Street. Turn left and walk forward, and on the right-hand side of the roadway can be seen some iron railings. Here until the Great Fire of London in 1666, was the **Parish Church of St. Peter West Cheap**. (25) The original foundation date for the church is unknown, but an early reference to the parish was made in 1231. Destroyed in the Great Fire the church was not rebuilt, and the parish was united with St. Matthew, Friday Street, on the other side of Cheapside. Early records refer to the church as being either "St. Peter at the Cross", referring to the Eleanor Cross in Cheap, or simply as "St. Peter West Chepe". From its important situation at the western end of "The Chepe" it received much attention from visiting personages. When Elizabeth I, 1533-1603, passed through the City in 1559 she paused at the church and the waites (singers) on the roof passed down to her, tied with a ribbon, a copy of the (New) English Bible. The Queen thanked them and "received it with both hands and kissed it, and clasped it to her bosom, and promised that she would read it diligently, to the great comfort of the bystanders."

All that is left of the church is a small portion of the churchyard which now forms one of the many open spaces of the City of London. On the rear wall of the shops in Cheapside there is to be found a stone tablet that reads "Erected at ye sole cost and charge of the parish of St. Peter, Cheape, Ao Dom. 1678". The London Plane tree, Platanus x hispanica, mentioned in Leigh Hunt's, 1784-1859, poem "The Town", published 1834 when the tree was fully grown still stands in the churchyard today. In the "Liber Albus" written at the time of Henry III, 1207-1272, the church is mentioned in connection with a murder that had taken place in St. Paul's churchyard. The entry reports that a man by the name of Geoffrey Russel witnessed there the stabbing of Ralph Wryvefuntaines, and being frightened that he would be accused of the murder, ran away. He took shelter (sanctuary) in St. Peter West Chepe. Here, in 1361, Nicholas Faringdon, a "man of mark", who was Mayor of the City four times, in 1308, 1313, 1320 and 1323, left money for the erection of a chantry chapel here for himself and family. Faringdon Street in the City remembers his name still today. In 1491 Thomas Wood, goldsmith and sheriff, is accredited with having either built or restored the roof of the middle aisle the corbels (roof supports) being carved as woodmen, it is said that the street received its name from the benefactor of this church. Others would have it otherwise. In his will 1503 Sir John Shaa or Shaw left money to rebuild the church.

> *"I wyll that my sayd executors shall cause the sayd church of St. Peter to be bylled and made wt a flatte roofe. And also the Stepull ther to be made up in gode and couenient manr"*

At the junction of Wood Street and Cheapside (26) stood one of the last **Eleanor Crosses** to be erected on the sites where Queen Eleanor's c. 1245-1290, body rested on its way to burial in Westminster Abbey. Here in addition to an 'over-night stay' on the journey, the queen's heart which had been removed during the embalming of her body in Lincoln, was removed from the hearse and sent, and buried, in Blackfriars Monastery, at the specific request of the queen. The cross became a centre for pilgrims visiting the City of London during the Middle Ages, but in 1581 it was defaced by the Puritans. "The image of Our Lady, (one of several saints depicted on the cross), was at that time robbed of her Son, and her arms broken by which she stayed Him on her knees". In the same year, 1581, Saint Edmund Campion and his companions passed by the Cross on their way to the Tower of London for imprisonment Although he was tightly bound on horseback, he made a low reverence to the Cross at the top of the memorial. Bystanders booed and hissed at him for this simple act of piety. It was in 1643 that John Evelyn, 1620-1706, English gentleman and diarist, recorded in his diary for 2nd May that year, "I went to London where I saw the furious and zealous people demolish that stately cross in Cheapside". A few days after the Cross had been finally removed the site was the scene of the burning of the Book of Sports—first published in 1618, and reissued by Charles I, 1600-1649—which listed those sporting activities that were permitted to take place on a Sunday. The Puritans of the later

17th century disapproved of ALL sports on the Sabbath, and consequently encouraged the destruction of these books. When the book first appeared the King, James I, 1566-1625, ordered that it should be read from every pulpit. But many of the clergy refused to do so, and the Order was withdrawn, only to re-appear under Charles I, 1600-1649.

Also to be found where **Wood Street** meets Cheapside (27) is a short row of shops, shown on some early maps as "The Long Shop", the present buildings date after the Great Fire of London 1666, but shops were first erected here in the early 15th century. Parochial records show that in 1401 the then parishioners bought the land and had the shops built, and the parish still receives rents from the site today!

On the corner of Cheapside and Foster Lane stands the **Parish Church of St. Vedast** (28).

One of only three churches dedicated to the 6th century saint in the country—the others being in Norwich (now only commemorated by a street name), and the other in Tathwell in Lincolnshire. Nobody has ever satisfactorily explained why there should have been any, let alone three, churches dedicated to this particular saint. The first mention of this church in London was in 1170, with John de Ruberge being noted as the first priest-in-charge, or rector, in 1291. A chaplain to Edward IV, 1442-1483, Father Thomas Rotherham, rector here in 1465, later became the Bishop of Rochester from 1468 to 1472 and was then translated to Lincoln where he stayed for eight years he became Archbishop of York in 1480 and remained there until his death in 1500. His tomb in York Minster (Cathedral) is now encased in a modern altar in the Chapel of St. Nicholas. On his death in 1532 John Brown, Sergeant Painter to Henry VIII, 1491-1547, left money in a bequest of 6s 8d a year in order that the Parish Clerk might arrange for the children of the parish to say the "De Profundis" each night at his family's tomb. He was buried in the church. The Parish Room was the meeting place for members of the Protestant Association, and it was here that Lord George Gordon arranged the meetings that led to the "No Popery" riots which started in St. George's Fields and which terrorized London during the 18th century.

We have now returned almost to the starting point for the walk, **New Change and Cheapside** (29).

Fleet Street—ink and martyrs' blood

Fleet Street—
ink and martyrs' blood

For hundreds of years Fleet Street has been closely associated with Printing—from the days in the 16th century, when it, and the area surrounding St. Paul's Cathedral, became the centre for book-publishing in London. In later times national and local newspapers were published here.

At the spot where the City of London meets the City of Westminster there stood until its removal in 1878, **Temple Bar** (1), the site of which is now marked by a memorial erected in 1880, to the designs of Sir Horace Jones, 1819-1887. The last Bar to be erected here was designed by Sir Christopher Wren, 1632-1723, now rests in a somewhat derelict state in the grounds of Theobalds Park in Hertfordshire. John Strype, 1643-1737, historian and biographer, and successor to John Stow, 1525-1605, the author of "A Survay of the City of London" published in 1598, writes of Temple Bar, as being "the place where the Freedom of the City of London and the Liberty of the City of Westminster doth part". Originally little more than a post or two, with a chain between them marking the boundary, while on occasions of City and National celebrations temporary structures would be erected to house, amongst other people the waits who would sing a welcome to the visitors to the City. Here both Elizabeth I, 1533-1603, and her half-sister Mary, 1516-1558, were greeted by the Lord Mayor of London and his entourage. The first stone structure was placed here after the Great Fire of 1666, in 1672 and was the one designed by Wren referred to earlier. It was never a fortified entrance to the City of London, but acted as a kind of frontier post at which potential visitors to the City could be stopped, and if necessary, turned away from entering London. It was also the place where the heads and limbs of those who had been executed were displayed—as a deterrent to others! Horace Walpole, 1717-1797, writing in 1746 tells us that "people make a trade of letting spying glasses at a half-penny a look" for a better view of these grisly remains. Today the traffic flows past the site, although somewhat impeded by the memorial in the centre of the roadway.

Shortly after entering Fleet Street, on the left hand side of the roadway, is **Chancery Lane** (2)—a few yards along which can be found the **Public Records Office** (3) which stands on the site of the Domus Conversorum, a House for converted Jews, that had been founded in 1232 by Henry III, 1207-1272, and in which the Dominican Friars looked after the needs of the converts, who at that time had their London house at the other end of the lane. They later moved into the City of London to an area still named Blackfriars. Although there seems to have been a considerable need for the House up to the 13th century, prior to the expulsion of the Jews in the later part of the same century by Edward I, 1239-1307. By the time of their return in the 17th century the house seems to have declined. When the Public Records office was established on the site the old chapel of the House was demolished, but some of the tombs were transferred to the new building. Here can still be seen the superb effigy of Dr. John Young, Master of the Rolls, 1467-1516 by Pietro Torrigiani, who was also responsible for the effigies of Henry VII, 1457-1509, and that of his queen, Elizabeth of York, who died in 1502, and was the first person to be buried in Henry VII's chapel in Westminster Abbey.

Return to Fleet Street, and cross the roadway and pass under **Prince Henry's Room** (4), a building erected in the 17th century as a meeting place for the Duchy of Cornwall's Council Chamber, and displaying the fleur-de-lis of the Prince of Wales, together with the motto "Ich Dien"—"I Serve" both outside and inside the building. Walk down Inner Temple Lane to the **Temple Church** (5) —now the place of worship for the Inner and Middle Temple inhabitants. Founded in 1185 as the church for the Order of the Holy Sepulchre of Knights Templars, commonly called "The Knights Templar", an Order founded in the 12th century in order to protect places in the Holy Land, Palestine, from the constant attacks of the Saracens. They settled in London at the north end of Chancery Lane, near to where Southampton Buildings now stands, and moved here at the end of the century. They were disbanded in the 14th century after they had become so powerful that even kings and emperors feared them. Their property here and elsewhere was handed over to their rivals in the Holy Land the Knights Hospitallers, who had their own property in Clerkenwell, and let the Temple to 'men of law and their students'.

The Temple church as it stands today is a reminder of the glory of the Order of the past. Here in the Round Church, can be seen the restored tombs of some of the early members of the Templars. The Templars, as well as the Hospitallers, built most of their churches round in deference to the Church of the Holy Sepulchre in Jerusalem that is built over the site of the Tomb of Christ. The 13th century additions to the church are still in constant use by members of both the Inner and Middle Temple whose pastoral needs are cared for by The Master of the Temple, an Anglican priest appointed by the Crown and not the Church.

While it is pleasant to wander around the lanes and courtyards of the Temple their place in London's history does not concern us here. We return to Fleet Street by way of **Inner Temple** Lane (6) through which we entered The Temple. Pause on our journey to remember Blessed Richard Langhorne, born in Bedford, he studied law in the Inner Temple, where he was visited by Titus Oates and was duly charged with being involved in the mythical Popish Plot which he, Oates, 1649-1705, concocted in 1678. Using knowledge that he had gained while pretending to study for the priesthood, Titus, together with Israel Tonge, a fanatical anti-Jesuit, plotted to overthrow Charles II, 1630-1685, and put the Duke of York, later James II, 1633-1702, on the Throne instead. With this accomplished Oates planned to burn London and to massacre the Protestants. After the plot had been discovered over thirty people were executed, but Oates himself escaped any form of punishment. Richard Langhorne was however found guilty of being concerned with "the plot" and hung, drawn and quartered at Tyburn on 14th July 1679.

Fleet Street (7) has been described as being one of the great historic highways of London with a number of Catholics living in it being reported to the Council and where in 1578 Mass was often heard at Baron Browne's house.

On the north side of the street stands the **Parish Church of St. Dunstan in the West** (8) which is first mentioned in 1237 when the

Abbot of Westminster, Richard de Barking gave the living to Henry III, 1207-1272, in order that the profits might be used for the recently established House for Jewish Converts in Chancery Lane. (qv). This was a reversal of the original gift of the land for the church at the time when St. Dunstan, c909-988 A.D., who was the Archbishop of Canterbury from 959 to 988 A.D., persuaded King Edgar, 944-975 A.D., to give the land to Westminster Abbey. Later, in 1361, the patronage once again changed hands. On this occasion the parish became the property of the Abbot of Alnwick in Northumberland, a Praemonstatensian Convent. After the convent was destroyed in the Scottish Wars of Independence one of the monks was deputed to serve as parish priest here in London. The medieval church was demolished in 1825, and the'new', present church was consecrated 31st July 1832, in order that Fleet Street might be widened. The church is octagonal in shape and is made up of seven recesses one of which, the north one, houses the altar for the church. Other recesses are used by members of the Orthodox churches, as well as the Coptic Church. There is also a shrine to the Polish Catholic Church here. It was, however, to the medieval church that two of the "Eleven Bishops", those bishops who were deprived of the Sees by Elizabeth I, 1533-1603, were buried. In 1559 Dr. Ralph Baines, (Bishop of Lichfield and Coventry, a noted Greek and Hebrew scholar a bishop defending the Catholic Faith at the Westminster Conference, was deprived of his Sees and confined for a time in the Palace of the Bishop of Lincoln, Nicholas Bullingham,) died in London and was buried here in the medieval church. The other bishop was Dr. Owen Oglethorpe, Bishop of Carlisle, who was the only member of the Marian hierarchy who would crown Elizabeth I. But he left the service before the Mass, with the rest of the bishops, after refusing to omit the Elevation of the Host at the Mass. A married priest was called upon to say the Mass, which he did, without the Elevation. Dr. Oglethorpe was also buried in the church in 1560. Records in the Public Records Office in Chancery Lane show a number of recusants living in the parish in the 17th century. The word 'recusant' is derived from the Latin *recuso* "I refuse", and was levied at all persons, Catholics and Non-conformists alike, who refused to attend service at the Church of England. The Albery family are shown in the records to have lived in the parish during the 17th century, one of whom is listed as being Thomas Albery, "father of priest, lately of Okingham (Wokingham) Berks," who in his Will left the tenement in Chancery Lane "where I did lately dwell . . ." and other bequests in Berkshire to "my grandchild Thomas, and the eldest son of my son Henry". Henry Albery is also mentioned in another Will, as being the brother of the priest, and leaving Lock's Farm House in the Parish of Wokingham, Berks, to his children, all of whom were minors at the time of his death in 1632. One of Henry's children, who died in 1660, made a Will dated 1st May 1658, and describes himself as being of Future Lane in the Parish of St. Dunstan in the West, and wishes to be buried in the parish church when I die. Within the parish in the 16th century a number of printers set up for business, among them was Richard Pynson, "King's Printer to Henry VIII", from whom he received a salary. At first he was paid £2 per annum, but this was later increased to £4. His sign was "The George next St. Dunstan's Churchyard", in the main he was a printer of law books, but many of his other books showed him to be among the best printers of his time. His Boccacio (1494) and his Morton Missal (1500), brought him high praise from all quarters. He also produced works by Chaucer, Skelton, Lydgate as well as Froisart and Aesop's Fables. It was he who introduced the Roman type to English printing. As the King's Printer it fell to him to print the King's (Henry VIII) tract against Martin Luther. When Richard Pynson died in 1530 he was succeeded at "The George" by Robert Redman, although the office of King's Printer was passed to Thomas Berthlet, at his printing works further down Fleet Street. In 1540 Berthlet published, but did not print, a copy of Thomas Cranmer's, 1489-1556, Bible, from Fleet Street. In turn Redman was followed at "The George" by William Middleton who, with several other printers of Fleet Street, found himself in trouble and brought before the Council in 1543 for having "printing off suche bokes as wer thowght to be unlawfull, contrary to the proclamation". He was committed to the Fleet Prison, but, after a fortnight released, and made to pay a fine as well as submitting a list of all the books and ballads that he had printed over the past three years.

Continue on the same side of the roadway as the church and soon Fetter Lane is reached.

The Fleet Street end of Fetter Lane was a popular place of execution in the 16th and 17th centuries. Here Blessed Christopher Bayles was brought from nearby Bridewell prison, where he had been hideously tortured, and on one day been suspended by his hands for twenty-four hours. A seminary priest from Durham, he was sent to England as a missionary, after being educated in Rome and Rheims, He was ordained in 1587 and found guilty in 1590 of being a priest, was hung, drawn and quartered here on 4th March. In the following year two more executions took place on this spot including that of Blessed Mountford Scott, a priest from Suffolk. After leaving Cambridge University where he studied at Trinity Hall, he went to Douai, and was later ordained in Brussels. Four times he was arrested and four times he escaped, but a thorough search was made for him in East Anglia and he was finally arrested and brought to London. He was hung, drawn and quartered on 1st July 1591. At the same time Blessed George Beesley, a priest from Lancashire, was also executed having been caught in the London area and imprisoned in the Tower of London where, in the Martin Tower he carved his famous inscription. One of the spectators at the execution, seeing the badly tortured body of the saint, called out "Is this the treason? I came to see traitors but instead I have seen saints". He was quickly ushered away from the scene and put in prison for his audacity. So perished two saints on the same day, and an innocent bystander spent some time imprisoned.

On the same side of the roadway as Fetter Lane is **Red Lion Court** (9) where in September 1794 Father Anthony Carroll was knocked down and mugged. He was taken to St. Bartholomew's Hospital in Smithfield where he died of his wounds. Between Bouverie Street and **Whitefriars Street** (10) was to be found, prior to the Dissolution of the Monasteries in the mid-16th century, the London home of the Whitefriars, or Carmelites. These friars formed the Brotherhood of the Order of the Most Blessed Mother of God and ever Virgin Mary of Mount Carmel. They were founded in 1155, although their claim to be the living link with the hermits of the Old Testament times had been aired from time to time. Their present home is at Aylesford in Kent, where they have restored the former monastic buildings, and have added to them over the past decades. At the Dissolution their buildings were quickly demolished and the stones used elsewhere in and around the City of London, but the sanctuary of the precinct was allowed to remain until 1697. By this time the area had become known as "Alsatia", and was heavily inhabited by all kinds of rogues and vagabonds. In 1895 a 14th century crypt was uncovered which is recorded on a plaque in Britton's Court off Whitefriars Street. It has, in the past, been possible to visit the crypt from Monday to Friday, but it is now in an area of development and an inquiry to the City Information Centre in St. Paul's Churchyard would be advisable.

Return to Fleet Street once more, and find the former **Daily Telegraph** (11) building on the north side of the roadway. They bought the site from the Diocese of Peterborough in 1863 and remained there until 1987. Here at Peterborough Court was the town house of the Abbots, later Bishops, of Peterborough one of whom was another of the "Eleven Bishops" referred to earlier, Dr. David Poole being bishop between 1556 and 1559 when he was deprived of the See. He is described by a former librarian at the cathedral as being "too faithful to the Pope to acknowledge the supremacy of Elizabeth, who, therefore, deprived him of his Bishopric".

At the Fleet Street end of Shoe Lane stood the **Fleet Street "Standard"** (12), which like its counterpart in Cheapside was a gathering point for the citizens of London who lived near to it. Here, as in the 'other place' executions took place in the 16th and 17th centuries. This "Standard" was also a conduit, and had been erected in 1478 "with figures of angels and sweetly sounding bells before them". Water from the Tyburn River was piped to the conduit daily, and on occasions of great joy, the birth of a new prince would 'run rich with wine', and for good measure a tun (vat) or two of wine would be placed nearby, in case the piped flow ran dry! Here too on 6th May 1590 was executed Blessed Edward Jones, a seminary priest from the Diocese of St. Asaph, who had been educated at Rheims and ordained in 1588. Noted for his zealous preaching he was condemned to death for being a priest, and over the gallows there was placed an inscription "For treason and favouring of foreign invasion". When he protested he was thrown off the scaffold that had been erected near "The Standard" "and the butchery began". Also on the scaffold with him was Blessed Anthony Middleton, a seminary priest from Yorkshire, who became covered with Blessed Edward Jones' blood, and such was the uproar of the crowd that he was taken from Fleet Street and martyred at Clerkenwell instead. On the south side of Fleet Street opposite Shoe Lane is Salisbury Court which leads to **Salisbury Square** (13). This is the site of the Inn (House) where the Bishops of Salisbury lodged whilst in London, the garden of which ran down to the River Thames. Salisbury House was one of the best of its kind along the river bank, and was used by King and Prince alike to house their important guests from time to time. The house remained in the possession of the Bishops until early in the reign of Elizabeth I, when it passed into the hands of Sir Richard Sackville. How and why has remained a mystery to this day. But bearing in mind how Elizabeth persuaded the Bishop of Ely to part with his house in Ely Place, one can but wonder what pressures were brought to bear on the Bishop of Salisbury at that time. It was, however, used by Cardinal Campeggio who stayed here during the divorce proceedings of Henry VIII. Today redevelopments in the square make it almost impossible to think of the area as being one of the most desirable places of the 16th century.

Part of the garden area of Salisbury House with "two tenements by the gate of Salisbury Place became the possessions of Godstone Abbey". Here lived Thomas Berthlet, the King's Printer, "for a fee". Next to the Bishop's house and gardens was the **Parish Church of St. Bride's, Fleet Street** (14).

One of the small compensations gained by the destruction of St. Bride's Church in the Second World War, 1939-1945, was that it enabled the archaeologists to make a thorough examination of the site. In so doing they found beneath the floor that Wren had built after the church had been destroyed in the Great Fire of London in 1666, traces of no less than six previous churches here. In addition, they found a tesselated floor from a Roman villa on the site, and the edge of the town ditch. Now in the crypt of the church can be seen centuries of development in a carefully laid out permanent exhibition. Medieval charnel houses were also discovered —vaults where the bones of persons previously buried in the churchyard above were carefully stored. It was not an uncommon occurrence for churchyards to be cleared of the bones of those persons who had no living relations, and at a time when the churchyard had become over-crowded. Dozens of coffins were also found buried underneath the Wren floor, and these were carefully examined, and have since been reburied in communal graves in other cemeteries in London. The church's patron saint, St. Bride, or St. Brigid, Bridget, was an Irish nun in the sixth century who founded a nunnery in Kildare, c450-c523, and whose feast day is the 1st February. In her native land, Ireland, she is revered only slightly less than St. Patrick himself, although there is little that can be written about her with certainty. She is accredited with a large number of miracles, including how on one occasion she turned water into beer! The greatest credit however, goes to the fact that she founded the first community for women in Ireland, and after her death, the Cult of St. Brigid spread throughout Europe, and latterly to the United States of America. In the Middle Ages the area surrounding the church was a sanctuary enjoying special rights which were certainly beneficial to Henry de Battle, who after he had killed Thomas de Hall in 1235, took refuge here. He later escaped from the sanctuary and fled the country never to be heard of again.

In the 16th century the Rector, John Taylor, alias Cardmaker was thrown into Newgate prison and charged with heresy. From there he was taken to Smithfield where he was burnt alive. On arrival he met with an old friend, a man named Warren at which point the Rector's friends felt that his courage would fail him when seeing his friend in the flames—it didn't. On reaching the place of his martyrdom John Taylor knelt down and prayed, and then kissed the stake, after which he took his friend's hands and they died together. There projected out over the street, near to the church, a signboard on which was displayed the Sun. This was the house where in 1500 Wynkyn de Worde, probably of Worth in Alsace, set up his printing press when he moved from the sign of the Red Pale in Westminster where he had been the partner of William Caxton, c1422-1491, the "Father of English Printing". It has been suggested that he made the move from Westminster to Fleet Street for one or two reasons. Firstly the former premises were no longer large enough to cater for all the work that he was doing at that time, and secondly, that he realised that it would be more profitable to be working where the booksellers had congregated—St. Paul's churchyard.

Research has shown that between the two areas of St. Paul's and Fleet Street some one hundred printers had set up their presses In Fleet Street they were to be followed by two dozen others before the end of the century. Across the roadway from the church now stands the public house "The Poppinjay", and nearby is to be found Poppins Court. Both are reminders that the Poppinjay was the sign of the Abbot of Cirencesters' Inn in the Middle Ages here. But as early as 1428 the abbot had ceased to live here, and the inn is listed in a Will of Roger Lardener, a baker and parishioner of St. Brides in which he leaves the house to William Lardener, his brother. However at the time of the English Reformation of the 16th century, and the Dissolution of the Monasteries in 1539, the inn was 'acquired' by Henry VIII.

Walk down Bride Lane and in so doing pass the site of the **Bishop of St. David's** London hostel (15) on the left hand side of the roadway. Unlike his near neighbour, the Bishop of Salisbury's house, the hostel did not have a frontage on the River Thames, but did have access to the River by way of the Fleet River that flowed alongside his garden.

Turn right at the junction of Bride Lane and New Bridge Street and walk along until the site of **Bridewell** (16) is reached. Note the head of Edward VI, 1537-1553, in the keystone of the building. Taking its name from the nearby well of St. Brides the site was originally used as a palace by Henry VIII, 1491-1547, but his son Edward VI had no use for it and gave it to the City of London to be used as a workhouse (the first of its kind in London). It was also used frequently as a prison and many Catholics were interred there and tortured for their Faith.

Return along new Bridge Street until **Ludgate Circus** (17) is reached. It was near here that Saint Polydore Plasden, a secular priest in the 16th century, lived and worked with his father in their shop that sold musical instruments made of horns. He regularly offered the Mass near here at a Catholic house in Holborn where he met Saint Edmund Gennings, who was also a priest, he had been brought up a Protestant, and was converted while serving as a page in the household of a Mr Sherwood. The two priests arranged to say Mass together on 8th November 1591 at the house of Mrs Wells in Grays Inn Fields. They were interrupted by the arrival of an antipapal party whom Saint Polydore Plasden made wait outside the door until the Mass was over. He then let them in and surrendered to them. All those in the room were arrested and tried at the King's Bench in Westminster Hall and found guilty of treason. Saint Edmund Gennings and Saint Swithun Wells were taken to Grays Inn and 'hung, drawn and quartered'—the rest of the group were taken to Tyburn where they suffered the same fate. Only Mrs Swithun Wells was not executed, but was sentenced to life imprisonment instead, she died in prison in 1602.

Cross the roadway, and, passing under the railway bridge walk up Ludgate Hill towards St. Paul's Cathedral.

Today **Ludgate Hill** (18) presents an entirely different scene to the one that would have presented itself in the 16th century. Gone is the famous "La Belle Sauvage" inn from where coaches left for all parts of the country, and where plays were performed in the innyard. Here Sir Thomas Wyatt, c1521-1541, soldier and leader of a revolt against Mary I, 1516-1558 (who like her mother Catherine of Aragon was a devout Catholic, and whose first act on becoming Queen in 1553 was to repeal the religious laws passed by her half-brother, Edward VI, 1537-1553) stayed at the inn following his abortive attempt to prevent Mary's marriage to Philip of Spain in 1554. Walk up the hill, cross the roadway called Old Bailey and shortly on the right hand side will be found a Corporation plaque marking the **site of Ludgate** (19).

According to one tradition the city gate received its name from King Lud, a somewhat mythical King of unknown origin. It is more likely to be derived from an Old English word 'ludda' or 'ludgeat' meaning postern, or 'back-door'. In later years, however, it was to take on a far more important role being the gate nearest to the cathedral, and at the end of the roadway that linked the City of London to Westminster. The contemporary statue of Elizabeth I, 1533-1603, now to be seen outside St. Dunstan-in-the-West churchyard, was to be found on the gateway, as were three figures, also at the same church which were claimed to be Kind Lud and two of his sons. These latter statues doubtless gave rise to the alternative suggestion as to the origin of the gate's name.

Hard by the site of Ludgate stands the **Parish Church of St. Martin** (20) which according to another tradition was first built by a British king Cadwalla in the 7th century. John Speed, c1552-1629, the historian and cartographer, says that he (Cadwalla) was buried here and his image great and terrible, triumphantly riding on horse-back artificially cast on brass, was placed on the West Gate of the City to the fear and terror of the Saxon. The church has been repaired and rebuilt since its original foundation whatever the date might be. The central painting of three that make up the triptych shows the patron saint of the church—St. Martin of Tours sharing his cloak with a beggar outside the city of Amiens. On the night of this event Martin had a dream in which Christ appeared to him and thanked him for the use of half of his cloak. " . . . naked and ye clothed me . . . insomuch as ye have done it unto one of the least of my brethren ye have done it unto Me . . . " as the Bible story relates Christ having told His disciples. Either side of the central panel the paintings show St. Gregory and St. Mary Magdalene, two other parishes now united with St. Martin's Ludgate. William Sevenoakes, (a foundling named after the place where he was found,) died in 1418, and was commemorated by a memorial in the church, but this perished in the Great Fire of 1666 and was not replaced. He was adopted by a citizen of London, and rose to be the Lord Mayor of London in 1418 the year of his death. Out of gratitude for the kindness that he himself had received he left money for the founding of a hospital for the poor and several Free Schools for the poor children of the City of London. It was in this church that the Knights Templars were brought to trial in 1312 which led to their being disbanded and their goods confiscated. The church is the parish church of the Worshipful Company of Stationers and Newspaper Makers whose Hall can be seen in **Stationers' Court** (21) behind the church.

The origins of the Stationers Company are shrouded in mystery, but one thing can be certain and that is they were operational long before the advent of printing in the 16th century. In 1403 they applied to the Court of Aldermen for authority to elect Wardens, and to make their own rules and regulations for the control of the craft of Writers of the Text Letter. Until this time the production of books has been in the hands of the monastic establishments, both in the City of London as well as in other parts of the country. They took their title from the medieval Latin word "stationarius" meaning a stall-holder as opposed to being an itinerant seller of goods. Under this name they were able to register their craft as an Art or Mystery in 1556 at the time of Philip and Mary, 1516-1558, the letter doubtless fully aware of the many seditious and heretical books that were being published at that time. One of the chief former functions of the Guild was to seize, and burn, all books that were considered to be unfit for public reading. Decisions regarding the heretical books were under the direct control of the Archbishop of Canterbury, and he, together with the Bishop of London, the Senior Bishop of Church after the two Primates, were given control over book prices, and who should be allowed to print them. Another great service which the Company instigated in the 16th century was the establishment of a "Copyright Register" whereby books entered at Stationers Hall were considered to be the legal property of the writer. It was not until 1912 that the first Copyright Act was placed on the Statute Book of this country. All writers both of yesterday and today have much to be grateful for this Company's work over the last four hundred years or more.

One way out of the court, under a modern office building, is into **Ave Maria Lane** (22). This takes its name from the fact that in medieval times, in the course of perambulations around the precincts of St. Paul's Cathedral, the Rosary was said and here the procession stopped and recited the "Ave Mary", "Hail Mary". From here it is a short walk to **St. Paul's Cathedral** (23) in whose medieval churchyard a number of executions took place.

For publishing the Bull of Excommunication (by nailing it to the Bishops gate) against the Queen (Elizabeth I), Blessed John Felton, a layman was condemned to death, and was 'hung, drawn and quartered' in St Paul's churchyard on 8th August 1570. Another martyr of the 16th century was Blessed Thomas Pormont, a seminary priest, born in Lincolnshire where he was brought up in the Protestant Faith, but after studying for a degree at Trinity Hall Cambridge, accepted the Catholic Faith and went on to study at Douai College. In 1587 he was ordained and shortly afterwards he returned to England and found lodgings in the City of London, near to the cathedral. Several times he was caught and managed to escape until finally he was placed in the "care" of Robert Topcliffe. At his trial he was found guilty of being a priest and sentenced to be 'hung drawn and quartered', the sentence being carried out in the churchyard of the cathedral close to where he had lived, on 20th February 1592.

All that remains of the medieval **St. Paul's Cathedral** (24) above ground can be seen on the south side of the present building consisting of part of the cloisters and chapter house. In the 16th century St. Paul's churchyard became the working and living area for both printers and booksellers, with legal books, religious books—the Holy Bible being the most popular publication—being printed and published alongside classical works, and other educational publications needed for the ever growing number of schools in and around the City of London. Members of the Stationers Company dominated the area, with several of them becoming Master of the Guild. Foreign books too were readily sold in the shops here, and as the publications increased so did the stream of visitors to the shops in an area already attracting a large number of people to it.

There are still a few bookshops in the vicinity to attract the visitor into them, and so the great tradition of the 16th century still prevails.

Temple Bar

Kalendar of London Martyrs

January	11th	William Carter	1584	Tyburn
	21st	Edward Stransham	1586	Tyburn
		(alias Transham, alias Barber)		
		Nicholls	1586	Tyburn
		(alias Devereux, vere Wheeler)		
	22nd	William Patenson	1592	Tyburn
	24th	William Ireland	1679	Tyburn
		(vere Ironmonger)		
		John Grove	1679	Tyburn
	31st	Richard (Thomas) Reynolds	1642	Tyburn
		Alban (Bartholomew)	1642	Tyburn
		Roe (Rowe)		
February	1st	Henry Morse	1645	Tyburn
	3rd	John Nelson	1578	Tyburn
	7th	Thomas Sherwood	1578	Tyburn
	12th	George Haydock	1584	Tyburn
		James Fenn	1584	Tyburn
		Thomas Hemerford	1584	Tyburn
		John Nutter	1584	Tyburn
		John Munden	1584	Tyburn
	17th	William Richardson	1603	Tyburn
		(alias Anderson)		
	18th	William Harrington	1594	Tyburn
		John Pibush	1601	Tyburn
	21st	Thomas Pormort	1592	St. Paul's Churchyard
		(alias Whitgift, White, Pryce and Meres)		
		Richard Williams	1592	Tyburn
		Robert Southwell	1595	Tyburn
	26th	Robert Drury	1607	Tyburn
	27th	Mark Barkworth	1601	Tyburn
		(alias Lambert)		
		Roger Filcock	1601	Tyburn
		(alias Arthur)		
		Anne Line	1601	Tyburn
March	2nd	Nicholas Owen	1606	Tower of London
	4th	Christopher Bales	1590	Fleet St.
		Nicholas Horner	1590	Smithfield
		Alexander Blake	1590	Gray's Inn Lane
	7th	John Larke	1544	Tyburn
		German Gardiner	1544	Tyburn
		John Ireland	1544	Tyburn
	19th	Thomas Ashby	1544	Tyburn

April	8th	John Goodman	1642	Newgate
	11th	George Gervaise	1608	Tyburn
	17th	Henry Heath	1643	Tyburn
	19th	James Duckett	1602	Tyburn
	20th	Richard Sergeant (alias Lea and Long)	1586	Tyburn
		William Thompson (alias Blackburn)	1586	Tyburn
		Thomas Tichborne	1602	Tyburn
		Robert Watkinson	1602	Tyburn
		Francis Page	1602	Tyburn
May	4th	John Houghton	1535	Tyburn
		Robert Lawrence	1535	Tyburn
		Augustine Webster	1535	Tyburn
		Richard Reynolds	1535	Tyburn
		John Haile	1535	Tyburn
	6th	Edward Jones	1590	Fleet Street
		Anthony Middleton	1590	Clerkenwell
	9th	Thomas Pickering	1679	Tyburn
	19th	Peter Wright	1651	Tyburn
	22nd	John Forest	1538	Smithfield
	28th	Margaret Pole	1541	Tower of London
		Thomas Ford	1582	Tyburn
		John Shert	1582	Tyburn
		Robert Johnson	1582	Tyburn
	30th	William Filby	1582	Tyburn
		Luke Kirby	1582	Tyburn
		Laurence Richardson (vere Johnson)	1582	Tyburn
		Thomas Cottam	1582	Tyburn
		William Scott	1612	Tyburn
June	1st	John Storey	1571	Tyburn
	6th	William Greenwood	1537	Newgate
	8th	John Davy	1537	Newgate
	9th	Robert Salt	1537	Newgate
	10th	Walter Pierson	1537	Newgate
		Thomas Green	1537	Newgate
	15th	Thomas Scryven	1537	Newgate
	16th	Thomas Redying	1537	Newgate
	19th	Humphrey Middlemore	1535	Tyburn
		William Exmew	1535	Tyburn
		Thomas Woodhouse	1573	Tyburn
	20th	Thomas Whitbread (alias Harcourt & Harcott)	1679	Tyburn
		William Harcourt (alias Waring, vere Barrow)	1679	Tyburn

		John Fenwick (vere Caldwell)	1679	Tyburn
		John Gavan	1679	Tyburn
		Anthony Turner	1679	Tyburn
	22nd	John Fisher	1535	Tower Hill
		Thomas More	1535	Tower Hill
	23rd	Roger Ashton	1592	Tyburn
		Thomas Garnet	1608	Tyburn
	28th	John Southworth	1654	Tyburn
	30th	Philip Powel (alias Morgan)	1646	Tyburn
July/		Thomas (Covert) Cort	1538	Newgate
August		Thomas Belchiam	1538	Newgate
	1st	Thomas Maxfield	1616	Tyburn
	1st/	Montford Scott	1591	Fleet St.
	2nd	George Beesley	1591	Fleet St.
	6th	Thomas Alfield	1585	Tyburn
		Thomas Webley	1585	Tyburn
	8th	John Griffith	1539	Southwark
		John (?) Waine (Maine)	1539	Southwark
	9th	Adrian Fortescue	1539	Tower Hill
		Thomas Dingley	1539	Tower Hill
	12th	David Gonson (Gunston)	1541	Southwark
		John Jones	1598	Southwark
	14th	Richard Langhorne	1679	Tyburn
	19th	Antony Broby (Brookby)	1537	Newgate
	26th	William Ward	1641	Tyburn
	30th	Thomas Abel	1540	Smithfield
		Edward Powell	1540	Smithfield
		Richard Fetherston	1540	Smithfield
	31st	Everard Hanse	1548	Tyburn
August	4th	William Horne	1540	Tyburn
		Edmund Brindholme	1540	Tyburn
		Clement Philpot	1540	Tyburn
	8th	John Felton	1570	St. Paul's
	9th	Richard Bere	1537	Newgate
	24th	Nicholas Tichborne	1601	Tyburn
		Thomas Hackshott (Hackshaw)	1601	Tyburn
	28th	William Dean	1588	Mile End Green
		Henry Webley	1588	Mile End Green
		William Gunter	1588	Shoreditch
		Robert Morton	1588	Lincoln's Inn Fields
		Hugh More	1588	Lincoln's Inn Fields
		Thomas Holford (alias Acton and Bude)	1588	Clerkenwell

		Name	Year	Place
	30th	Richard Leigh (alias Garth or Earth)	1588	Tyburn
		Edmund Shelley	1588	Tyburn
		Richard Martin	1588	Tyburn
		Richard Flower (vere Lloyd or Floyd	1588	Tyburn
		John Roche (alias Neale)	1588	Tyburn
		Margaret Ward	1588	Tyburn
Sept.	7th	John Duckett	1644	Tyburn
		Ralph Corby (vere Corbington)	1644	Tyburn
	20th	Thomas Johnson	1537	Newgate
Oct.	5th	William Hartley	1588	Shoreditch
		Robert Sutton	1588	Clerkenwell
		John Hewitt (alias Weldon and Savell)	1588	Mile End Green
	8th	John Lowe	1586	Tyburn
		John Adams	1586	Tyburn
		Robert Dibdale	1586	Tyburn
	12th	Thomas Bullaker	1642	Tyburn
	19th	Philip Howard	1595	Tower of London
Nov.	24th	Edward Mico (alias Harvey)	1678	Wild House London
Dec.	1st	Edmund Campion	1581	Tyburn
		Robert Sherwin	1581	Tyburn
		Alexander Briant	1581	Tyburn
	3rd	Edward Coleman	1678	Tyburn
	5th	John Almond	1612	Tyburn
	10th	Edmund Gennings	1591	Gray's Inn Fields
		Swithun Wells	1591	Gray's Inn Fields
		Eustace White	1591	Tyburn
		Polydore Plasdon	1591	Tyburn
		Brian Lacey	1591	Tyburn
		John Mason	1591	Tyburn
		Sidney Hodgson	1591	Tyburn
	10th	Thomas Somers (alias Wilson)	1610	Tyburn
		John Roberts	1610	Tyburn
	11th	Arthur Bell	1643	Tyburn
	12th	Thomas Holland (alias Sanderson and Hammond)	1642	Tyburn
	21st	Thomas Bedingfeld (alias Mumford, vere Downes)	1678	Gatehouse Westminster
	29th	William Howard	1680	Tower Hill

Glossary